THE
GOD
of all
COMFORT

D1024073

Devotions of hope for those who chronically suffer

THE
GOD
of all
COMFORT

JUDY GANN

LIVING
INK
BOOKS
Writing Worth Reading

ISBN 0-89957-155-7

First printing—March 2005

Cover designed by Mike Meyers, Meyers Design, Shepherd, Texas
Interior design and typesetting by Reider Publishing Services,
    West Hollywood, California
Edited and proofread by Christy Phillippe, Dan Penwell, Sharon Neal,
    and Warren Baker

Printed in the United States of America
11 10 09 08 07 06 05 –RO– 8 7 6 5 4 3 2 1

In memory of Donna Creelman Gann—
not a day goes by when you don't come to mind,

and in honor of Joe Gann—
who still never lets a week go by without calling,

and my parents—my greatest cheerleaders.

Contents

CONTENTS

CONTENTS

CONTENTS

SECTION 8
Eyes toward Heaven

Acknowledgments

The writing of *The God of All Comfort* was a treacherous eight-year journey. Yet, each step of the way, God surrounded me with support and encouragement. My deepest thanks to:

My writing prayer team: *Dick & June Anderson, Sue Bakken, Morri DeWitt, Marlene Etter, Margie Harris, Ruth Knutson, Kathi Loverin, Chris & Sarah Mechler, Dorothy Parrish, Nancy Shaffer*, and *Alice Watkins*. As Oswald Chambers said, "Prayer does not fit us for the greater work; prayer *is* the greater work." Your prayers were the "greater work" and sometimes all that kept me writing.

The people who shared their stories with me: My name may be on the cover, but much of the heart of *The God of All Comfort* comes from your generosity and vulnerability in sharing how God comforts you in your health struggles.

Terri Paske: Your question started it all! I hope my answer encourages you.

Lura Anderson & Cathy Miller: You recognized God's gift and encouraged me to use it.

Nancy Shaffer: Your bookstore manager perspective and feedback (plus all the lattes!) were invaluable in the early days of writing my manuscript.

Peggy King Anderson: Thank you for critiquing my first attempts. I hope you see vulnerability and word pictures in the finished product.

Stacey Padrick: You paved the way before me, giving me courage to pursue my dream in spite of my illnesses. God always gave you just the words to say to me.

Lisa Copen: You are my inspiration! Your support means more than you'll ever know.

Tricia Goyer: Editing my manuscript before the final submission was an incredible gift. Your words, "Remember, Judy, God already sees the finished book," echoed in my mind during the last difficult months of this project.

Wendy Lawton: For your mentoring, hand holding and gentle nudges when I needed them.

The faculty and conferees at the Mount Hermon and Oregon Christian Writers Conferences: I had the passion. You gave me the tools, support, and networking opportunities to make this book a reality.

Dan Penwell: My editor and friend—a gift from God. You championed this book years before it existed. Thank you for walking me along this new path. Every first-time author should be so blessed!

Christy Phillippe, Dan Penwell, Sharon Neal, and *Warren Baker*: Your editorial skills strengthened my writing—and made me sound so much better.

The incredible *publishing team at AMG*: Thank you for the contributions each of you made to the publishing and marketing of this book.

Pastor Jim & Jaci Kennington and my Lake City Community Church family: Your teaching, fellowship, prayers, and words of encouragement nurture me as a writer.

My dear family: *Dad, Peggy, Ryan, Allison, and Bailee*: Your love and long distance cheers ring in my heart.

And to the God of all comfort, to whom I owe it all.

Introduction

J udy, which Scripture passages comfort and encourage you when you're battling poor health?" asked Terri. "I'd like to share them with a friend who is ill."

Terri's question and my subsequent search through the Bible stayed in my mind long after I had provided her with a list of verses. And years later, her question motivated me to write this book you now hold in your hands.

I know the pain and limitations of illness. For over twenty years, I've suffered from fibromyalgia and other autoimmune system disorders. I was diagnosed and treated for breast cancer in 1994.

Fifteen years ago, I began to keep a journal of my devotional times with the Lord. Exhausted and hurting, I cried out to God on the pages of these journals, and I recorded God's answers through his Word in them as well. Much of what you'll read in this book originated in these journal entries.

But I didn't want to limit *The God of All Comfort* to just my own narrow experiences with illness. Seventeen other people opened their hearts and shared their stories within the pages of this book. They suffer from a variety of illnesses, including cancer, arthritis, and lupus. I pray you will recognize yourself in our struggles and feel less alone in your pain.

Illness breeds physical, spiritual, and emotional devastation. When we're sick and hurting, pain and fatigue scream for our attention. Fear and doubt take root in our hearts and minds. Questions about suffering tear at the fabric of our Christian faith. Daily we deal with issues such as pain, weakness, loss of independence, loneliness, and the reality of death.

My prayer is that these devotionals will draw you into God's Word to find the comfort, strength, and hope you need to cope with the challenges of living with illness. We aren't left to struggle on our own. Our loving, compassionate heavenly Father is the source of all comfort. Within the pages of the Bible are his promises of strength, hope, *and* his presence.

I pray you will come away from reading these devotionals strengthened, renewed, and trusting in the "God of all comfort" for each step of your journey with illness.

Praise be to the God and Father of our Lord Jesus Christ, the Father of compassion and the God of all comfort, who comforts us in all our troubles, so that we can comfort those in any trouble with the comfort we ourselves have received from God. (2 Cor. 1:3, 4)

By God's Design

The LORD will fulfill his purpose for me;

your love, O LORD, endures forever—

do not abandon the works of your hands.

—PSALM 138:8

Wonderfully Made

For you created my inmost being;
you knit me together in my mother's womb.
I praise you because I am fearfully and wonderfully made;
your works are wonderful,
I know that full well. (Ps. 139:13, 14)

Swollen and red, the joints in my hands throb. As I move, muscle pain spreads throughout my body. Weakness and fatigue render me virtually useless. On this beautiful spring morning, I feel anything but "fearfully and wonderfully made." Did God make a mistake?

Sometimes I dream about what it would be like to possess a healthy body. I'd walk across the room without stopping to rest. I wouldn't have to hoard my energy. Dressing wouldn't be such a painful hassle. Bending to retrieve books from a shelf would be an almost effortless task. Sometimes it's difficult to believe that "my frame was not hidden" from my Creator, the God of the universe, "when I was made in the secret place" (Ps. 139:15). It's hard to fathom that my Creator had a plan in mind when he formed me.

In my limited understanding, I view my pain as a knotty hindrance. However, God sees a different picture, a complete picture. He sees my weaknesses as essential threads in the unique tapestry he is creating of my life.

Not until my life, your life, is finished and silent, will we understand the darker threads of our human tapestries and their contribution to the beauty of our unique design.

We may disagree with God's choice of colors. But we are works in progress—still stretched on God's loom.

> *Father, as I lie here weak and hurting, I choose to praise you for the wonderful ways in which you have knit me together. Thank you that my pain and my weakness are valuable in your design of my life.*

My life is but a weaving
Between my Lord and me;
I cannot choose the colors,
He worketh steadily.

Ofttimes He weaveth sorrow,
And I in foolish pride,
Forget He sees the upper,
And I the underside.

Not 'til the loom is silent
And the shuttles cease to fly,
Shall God unroll the canvas
And explain the reason why.

The dark threads are as needful
In the Weaver's skillful hand,
As the threads of gold and
    silver,
In the pattern He has planned.

—AUTHOR UNKNOWN

In God's Eyes

"Since you are precious and honored in my sight,
and because I love you,
I will give men in exchange for you,
and people in exchange for your life." (Isa. 43:4)

"The LORD your God is with you,
he is mighty to save.
He will take great delight in you,
he will quiet you with his love,
he will rejoice over you with singing." (Zeph. 3:17)

J anine shivered and wrapped her thick black coat tightly around her. For over an hour, she peered through the glass door of the auditorium, eager to catch a glimpse of her children as they performed in the school Christmas concert. *Lord, I feel like a leper. Must I always be on the outside looking in?*

Because Janine suffers from MCS (multiple chemical sensitivity), she is unable to tolerate the whiffs of fragrances swirling through the auditorium. Migraines, seizures, blurred vision, and debilitating fatigue assault Janine whenever she's exposed to these chemicals. Pesticides and new carpets are also a problem. But it makes matters worse when others have a hard time understanding her situation.

In a culture that loathes blemishes, there is little room for those who aren't "perfect." The value of those who suffer from illness is often perceived as less, yet that couldn't be farther from the truth.

In the eyes of God, we are precious jewels. God delights in us. He purchased us with the sacrificial blood of his own Son. His love for us is unconditional—not based on our abilities and achievements—or our health.

When our worth is measured according to worldly standards, we may feel like outcasts—peering in the windows of the lives of others who can do more. But looking through the eyes of God, regardless of our state of health, we are cherished treasures, over whom he rejoices with singing.

Father, thank you for your unconditional love and acceptance. Help me to view others and myself through your eyes.

"Instead of looking into the mirror of other people's opinions about us, we constantly need to look into the mirror of God's love for us—a love that is unconditional, accepting, extraordinary. If I look into that mirror, instead of being worried about my 'self-worth,' I'll have 'God-worth,' which is *so much better*."[1]

—RUTH MYERS

Who Am I Now?

*How great is the love the Father has lavished
on us, that we should be called children of God!
And that is what we are!* (1 John 3:1)

Mary Beth eased her body onto the park bench as her two toddlers scampered off to play with the other young children. Surveying the play area, she realized she was the only mom sitting on a bench. Mary Beth ached with envy as she watched mothers run, catch balls, and help their children—and hers—slide down the slide.

Idle on the bench because of chronic foot and calf pain, Mary Beth inwardly questioned her ability to fulfill the more physical aspects of her role as a good mom. *A good mom should run and play with her children. She should participate in her children's activities.* The pain of complex regional pain syndrome and its accompanying crutches and wheelchair threatened to strip Mary Beth of pieces of her treasured identity—a mother.

Most of us with chronic or serious illnesses face an identity crisis. In our culture, we tend to define our identity by our various roles: mother, father, teacher, lawyer, etc. Then along comes an illness, and suddenly we're robbed of our positions. Our image of ourselves becomes embedded in a disease. We struggle to adapt to the illness that overwhelms our lives. We look in the mirror and see the ravages of illness staring back at us. We wonder—*who am I now?*

Amid the rubble of our shattered selves, we still possess the one identity that truly matters. This identity is untouched by disease. Medication and fatigue can't alter it. This is the identity we have in Christ. In him we are children of God.

In his infinite love, God, our heavenly Father, adopted us into his family. Because of our relationship with his Son, Jesus Christ, we are God's cherished children. No illness can rip this identity from us.

Chronic illness remolds our lives. Pain distorts our self-images. But although we may wonder who we are, we need never wonder *whose* we are. We are the beloved children of God, and as Jesus said, "No one can snatch them out of my Father's hand" (John 10:29).

> *Father, I thank you that I'm your adopted child. When pain warps my image of myself, remind me that I'm a child of the King.*

Yet to all who received him, to those who believed in his name, he gave the right to become children of God. (John 1:12)

A Purpose in Pain

And we know that in all things God works for the good of those who love him, who have been called according to his purpose. (Rom. 8:28)

Rigid with fear, Belinda sat in the doctor's office awaiting the verdict. For weeks she'd endured an endless battery of painful and exhausting tests. *What's going to happen to me? Why won't the doctors tell me anything? They must know something!*

Nothing she'd imagined prepared Belinda for her diagnosis: multiple sclerosis. The words screamed in her ears, while at the same time her mind refused to comprehend them. *The test results are wrong. Surely the doctors made a mistake. How can I fix this?*

Belinda's marriage was shaky before her diagnosis. Now faced with the reality of a serious debilitating disease, her life crumbled. Belinda felt utterly alone. Uncontrollable sobs wracked her body.

During this time of despair, God surrounded Belinda with Christians. These Christian friends prayed for her and talked to her about the Lord. They shared how he would be with her, no matter what. But she couldn't understand why Jesus would save her. What had she ever done for him?

It took Belinda a long time to see salvation as a gift from God through the sacrificial death of his Son—to realize Jesus died for her. Once she understood, Belinda prayed, confessed her sins, and accepted Christ as her Savior.

This isn't the end of her story. God was also working in the heart of Belinda's husband. Within hours of Belinda's acceptance of Jesus, he became a Christian, too. Reunited in Christ, they desired God's direction in their marriage and family. In sickness or in health, she and her husband placed their future in God's hands.

Belinda's illness didn't disappear when she became a Christian. Multiple sclerosis is a horrific disease. Some days are tough and her tears flow freely. Yet Belinda no longer travels through the valley of illness alone. Jesus walks with her. Like Joseph whose brothers left him for dead, Belinda can say, "But God intended it for good" (Gen. 50:20). As God used the cruelty of Joseph's brothers to accomplish his good for Israel, God used her illness to draw Belinda and her husband to himself and to each other.

God can remove our illnesses and change our circumstances in an instant—the moment they are no longer needed for his divine purposes. Until then, or until he takes us home, we can rest in the fact that our illnesses are part of his good purpose for our lives. God truly uses *all* things.

Thank you, Lord, that you are the blessed controller of my life. Help me to trust you to use all that happens to me for my ultimate good.

"When we surrender ourselves to whatever process God chooses to make us more like Him, we can abide in Christ in any circumstance for the glory of God."[2]

—CYNTHIA HEALD

For God's Glory

As he went along, he saw a man blind from birth.
His disciples asked him, "Rabbi, who sinned,
this man or his parents, that he was born blind?"
"Neither this man nor his parents sinned," said Jesus,
"but this happened so that the work of God might
be displayed in his life." (John 9:1–3)

My heart plunged when I recognized Julie's distinctive handwriting. Why bother even opening the envelope? Clothed in different words, the message in her letters was always the same: I must have unconfessed sin in my life. Otherwise, I would not be sick.

Julie's words always devastated me. They fueled my own guilt. *Is this illness my fault? Is it the result of some sin I had committed?* I probed my thoughts and my actions. A perfect link between an unconfessed sin and my illness eluded me.

In Jesus' day, people were grappling with the sickness-equals-sin issue, too. According to the Jewish culture, sickness was a direct result of sin. In the case of the man who had been blind since birth, the well-meaning disciples assumed his blindness was the result of sin, either his own or that of his parents.

In his answer to the disciples, Jesus identifies another reason for suffering. The man's blindness occurred so that God would be glorified. God was demonstrating his power in the life of the blind man. What a graphic testimony of God's glory to all who were watching him!

Although we live in a fallen world where sin and suffering abound, illness is not necessarily the result of sin. Sometimes God allows illness to invade our lives for a higher purpose. He knows what is best for each of us—what will bring him the greatest glory.

The next time you or someone else blames your illness on sin, prayerfully examine your heart. Your illness may provide the backdrop on which God displays his most glorious work.

Heavenly Father, help me to view my illness from your perspective. In sickness or in health, may my life bring great glory to you.

"Every trial that You [God] allow to happen is a platform on which You reveal Yourself, showing Your love and power, both to me and to others looking on."[3]

—RUTH MYERS, *31 DAYS OF PRAISE*

A Temple of God's Spirit

*Do you not know that your body is a temple of the Holy Spirit,
who is in you, whom you have received from God? You are
not your own; you were bought at a price. Therefore
honor God with your body.* (1 Cor. 6:19, 20)

J udy, you really should take better care of yourself," chided
Carol. "After all, your body is a temple of God's Spirit."

The truth of Carol's words cut deep. Times of illness force
me to make healthy choices. But I resume careless habits when
I'm enjoying a respite from disease. I become casual about what
I feed my body. I don't ration my energy. It's easy to stretch the
limits of my need for rest. And soon I'm caught in the downward spiral of illness.

However, as Carol reminded me, I am the *tenant*, not the
landlord, of this dwelling known as my body. God purchased me
with the priceless blood of Christ, his Son. As the tenant, I have
a responsibility to honor God with my body.

How do we honor God with our less-than-perfect bodies?
The key lies in viewing our bodies from God's perspective. We
tend to see our dwellings as sickly, weak, and worthless. But in

God's eyes, we are precious. Life is a gift. God has placed his Spirit within us.

A clear understanding of our bodies as God's vessels motivates us to eat balanced meals. Rest and exercise become tools for maintaining healthy dwellings for God's Spirit.

By worldly standards, our broken and weary outer shells bear no resemblance to temples. But we are the chosen sanctuaries of God's Spirit. When we practice healthy habits, we honor God and glorify him with our bodies.

> *Father, thank you for the gift of your Spirit. Help me to be a responsible tenant of the body you have entrusted to me.*

"When the possessor of heaven and earth brought you into being and placed you in this world, He placed you here not as owner but as a steward."[4]

—JOHN WESLEY

Unfinished Portrait

*Being confident of this, that he who began a good
work in you will carry it on to completion
until the day of Christ Jesus.* (Phil. 1:6)

The artist studies the blank canvas stretched across the frame. His eyes travel from the canvas to his subject and back again. With great deliberation and skill, he chooses and mixes the colors on his palette.

This is not a hurried task. Keeping his vision of the completed portrait in mind, the artist painstakingly outlines his composition on the canvas. With firm brushstrokes, he paints in the details of the portrait. The artist refuses to lay down his paintbrush until the portrait on the canvas matches the portrait in his mind.

We are like the unfinished portrait on the canvas. Pain, fatigue, and despair are among the shades of colors waiting on the palette. Relief from pain, renewed strength, and hope are also on the palette.

God, the Master Artist, grasps the paintbrush in his hand. Because he intends that our finished portraits be Christlike,

God blends precise tones of pain and joy into the portraits of our lives.

There are times when we loathe our portraits-in-progress. The dark tones of illness seem like blemishes on the canvas. We yearn for the day when our portraits will be completed. Yet it is reassuring to know that God continues to work on our life portraits. He applies blotches of pain and illness to make us more like Christ.

God's portraits will take our lifetimes to finish. Meanwhile, we can trust in his promise to complete the spiritual masterpieces he is creating of our lives. God will not lay down his paintbrush until his work in us is finished—on the day he calls us home.

Father, thank you for the work you are doing in my life. Forgive my impatience with the process. Help me to view the more painful brushstrokes as giving a beautiful texture to your finished masterpiece.

"There has never been the slightest doubt in my mind that the God who started this great work in you would keep at it and bring it to a flourishing finish on the very day Christ Jesus appears." (Phil. 1:6 The Message)

Strength for the Journey

Blessed are those whose strength is in you,

who have set their hearts on pilgrimage.

—PSALM 84:5

Strength for the Journey

Whom have I in heaven but you?
And earth has nothing I desire besides you.
My flesh and my heart may fail,
but God is the strength of my heart
and my portion forever. (Ps. 73:25, 26)

The mysterious illness sucked Marilyn's strength and vitality like a vacuum. Weakness infiltrated her body. Stripped of her usual good health, Marilyn no longer possessed the energy or the desire to fulfill the demands of her ministry. Discouragement and fear took root deep within her heart as Marilyn's life journey took an unwelcome turn.

Illness saps not only our physical strength, but also our spiritual and emotional energy. Depleted of all reserves, we become feeble in heart as well as body. Where can we find strength for the journey when our meager wells of energy have run dry?

Strength is not something we can manufacture, purchase, or ingest like a pill. It is a gift from God. His strength often comes wrapped in the packages of weakness and pain. It arrives when our own strength fails—when we've exhausted all other sources.

We tap into God's strength when we recognize our dependence on him. Sometimes God brings us to the end of our own puny strength so we will rely on his power. We can rest and relax in him, knowing that he is the one source of strength that never fails us.

God, in his wisdom, does not always supply physical strength for our journey. Instead he imparts the strength to persevere—to stand firm in the midst of difficult circumstances. This gift of endurance is the most potent strength of all.

The journey of chronic illness is long and treacherous. It demands every ounce of physical, emotional, and spiritual strength we can muster. At times our "flesh" and our "hearts" will fail. But as we draw on God's strength, he will meet our needs—every step of the journey.

Lord, sometimes I feel so weak and my journey seems so long. Thank you for the gift of your strength that will never fail.

"You were wearied by all your ways, but you would not say, 'It is hopeless.' You found renewal of your strength, and so you did not faint." (Isa. 57:10)

Daily Battles

"Your Father already knows your needs. He will give you all you need from day to day." (Luke 12:30, 31 NLT)

I can do everything through him who gives me strength. (Phil. 4:13)

The shrill ringing of the alarm clock yanked me out of a troubled sleep. *It can't be morning already!* Struggling into an upright position, I winced as pain penetrated every fiber of my being. My body was one giant headache.

As I lay in bed dreading the start of a new day, I rehearsed that day's to-do list in my mind. Go grocery shopping. Practice story time. Vacuum the living room. Do the laundry. Finish my Bible study. I fought an intense desire to retreat back under the covers. Surely my trickle of strength would evaporate long before I completed my tasks!

On mornings like this, I need to turn to the Lord, the source of my strength. For me, this includes surrendering my to-do list to him in prayer.

That infamous word *priorities* demands my attention. Are the items on my to-do list God's priorities, or mine? I hasten to align my list with God's.

In Philippians 4:13, the strength for "everything" is not the ability to complete *our* daily to-do lists. It's the ability to accomplish all that *God* has planned for us that day.

God's strength is supplied daily. We can't steal (or borrow!) from tomorrow's supply of strength in order to perform today's tasks. All we have is today.

Most of us with illness battle fatigue on a daily, even hourly basis. We know better than most that our own strength is not enough. On a *good* day, we may only accomplish one or two of our own planned tasks.

However, as we commit our tasks to the Lord, he will provide sufficient strength for each responsibility he assigns to us. In God's strength we find the power to face our daily battles.

Heavenly Father, thank you that I don't need to worry about the things I'm unable to finish today. Thank you that in your Son, I have the strength to accomplish all you ask me to do.

"To be honest, sometimes I want to forget it all and crawl back into bed. But a small voice inside of me says, 'Emilie, you don't have to do it all at once. Just put your feet on the floor and take the first step of the day.' "[1]

—EMILIE BARNES

Blessing in a Thorn

*To keep me from becoming conceited because of these
surpassingly great revelations, there was given to me a thorn
in my flesh, a messenger of Satan, to torment me. Three
times I pleaded with the Lord to take it away from me. But
he said to me, "My grace is sufficient for you, for my power
is made perfect in weakness." Therefore I will boast all the
more gladly about my weaknesses, so that Christ's power may
rest on me. That is why, for Christ's sake, I delight in weaknesses,
in insults, in hardships, in persecutions, in difficulties.
For when I am weak, then I am strong. (2 Cor. 12:7–10)*

I watched as my energetic coworker darted through the children's area. Familiar pangs of jealousy pricked my heart. I yearned for even a smidgen of my coworker's vitality.

Why am I burdened with this frail and broken body? If I were healthy, I could accomplish so much more for the Lord. Once again I begged God to heal me. Once again he answered, "No."

The thorn of chronic illness stings. Not only does physical pain hurt, but also the pain of limitations and weakness smarts, too. Often my reservoir of strength is depleted long before a task is finished. To me, chronic illness hinders my ability to use my God-given gifts and talents.

God gave Paul profound visions and revelations. What awesome gifts! What a temptation to exalt himself rather than God. But Paul's thorn deflated any tendency toward conceit. It is tough to be self-sufficient when wracked with pain.

God didn't remove Paul's thorn. Instead God redirected Paul's focus from the stinging thorn to the blessing of recognizing God's strength in his weakness. Humbled, Paul realized he was strongest when he was most dependent on God.

Paul did not "delight" in his thorn. He "delighted" in the power of God's strength infusing his weakness. Paul understood that his life was a "living demonstration of Christ's power" (2 Cor. 12:9 TLB).

I'm glad Paul didn't disclose the exact nature of his thorn. Because he wasn't specific, I can recognize similarities between Paul's situation and mine. Like Paul, I tend to think of myself as self-sufficient. God gave me unique gifts and abilities. On a "good day," I battle the temptation to rely on my own resources. Pride trespasses into my heart.

Without the thorn of chronic illness, I would miss the daily blessing of drawing on God's strength. When I exhaust my own resources, my thorn spurs me to trust solely in God's power.

Those of us coping with illness lack the stamina of a healthy person. Yet God's enabling power is most evident in our weakest moments. We experience the reality of God's promise when he says, "My power shows up best in weak people" (2 Cor. 12:9 TLB).

Father, thank you for the thorn of chronic illness. Without my thorn, I wouldn't know the blessing of relying on your strength. When my thorn stings, remind me that your grace and strength are sufficient. Your power shines brightest in my weakness.

To this end I labor, struggling with all his energy, which so powerfully works in me. (Col. 1:29)

The Tortoise and the Hare

*" 'Not by might nor by power, but by my Spirit,'
says the Lord Almighty." (Zech. 4:6)*

My favorite Aesop's fable is the story of "The Tortoise and the Hare." In this ironic tale, the flashy Hare boasts that he's the fastest runner in the land. Tired of Hare's bragging, Tortoise challenges Hare to a race.

As this mismatched race begins, Hare bolts for the finish line. Believing he has left Tortoise eating his dust back at the starting line, the overconfident Hare stops for a nap. Meanwhile, Tortoise inches along at a slow but steady pace. Tortoise tiptoes past the sleeping Hare and plods toward the finish line. By the time Hare awakens from his nap and darts to the finish, he's too late. Tortoise has already ambled over the line.

I love this example of persistence over power. Much of the time I trudge through the day, barely able to put one foot in front of the other. But the lesson of this fable is "slow and steady is the pace, slow and steady wins the race."

God delivers a similar message about strength through the prophet Zechariah. The remnant of Jews returned to Judah to rebuild the temple. At times their assignment seemed like a monumental task. Zechariah delivered an encouraging message to the disheartened people. He told them that true strength is not found in physical power or toughness, but in God's Spirit working within them, providing inner strength: the strength to persevere—one step at a time.

Throughout Scripture, God challenges his people to press on regardless of their circumstances. Faithful plodders include Abraham, Joseph, Moses, Joshua, David, and Paul. Weak in their own strength, they persevered in God's power.

Illness looms as a continual challenge—much like Tortoise's race with Hare. But in the strength of God's Spirit, we can shuffle toward the finish line. Step by step—just like Tortoise.

Lord, thank you for the spiritual strength you provide daily. When I want to quit the race, help me to persevere in your strength.

"When God wants to move a mountain, He does not take a bar of iron, but He takes a little worm. The fact is, we have too much strength. We are not weak enough. It is not our strength that we want. One drop of God's strength is worth more than all the world."[2]

—DWIGHT L. MOODY

The View from the Top

It is God who arms me with strength
and makes my way perfect.
He makes my feet like the feet of a deer;
he enables me to stand on the heights. (Ps. 18:32, 33)

The setting sun splashed shades of orange, red, tan, and black along the canyon walls. Lucy absorbed the exquisite vistas from the high, flat tableland that makes up the rim of the Grand Canyon.

Just walking from the tour bus to the rim was an arduous journey for Lucy. She suffers from sarcoidosis—a disease that can attack any organ of the body, particularly the lungs. Although awed by the beauty surrounding her, she fought for air—a rare commodity at the 7,000-foot-high south rim of the Grand Canyon.

Eager to observe the canyon from below, Lucy rested and then hiked about one hundred feet down the foot trail leading to the raging Colorado River at the canyon floor. She enjoyed the view before turning and starting her journey back up to the rim of the canyon.

Each upward step threatened to steal Lucy's breath. Her legs trembled as she searched for the next solid foothold. Even the smallest step sucked her tiny portion of strength. Hours seemed to pass before, at last, her feet were firmly planted back on the rim of the Grand Canyon.

Living with illness is like ascending a steep mountain path. We stumble along the treacherous terrain of pain and fatigue. At times we doubt we can take another step. The top of the mountain stretches high above our reach. The temptation to just let go and slide to the bottom of the hill tantalizes us.

We don't scale this mountain alone. God may not eliminate our rough roads and mountainous circumstances. But he accompanies us on the upward journey, marking the road before us. He provides us with the strength to stand firm and climb above our difficulties.

With our feet anchored in God's footprints, we can climb with the sure, steady pace of a deer. Breath by breath. Step by step. In his strength, we stand on the high places. Oh, what a beautiful view!

> *Lord, thank you for giving me the strength to climb this high, rough road of illness. Keep my feet from slipping, and help me to stand firm and steady in you.*
>
>

"You can't understand why the road doesn't get easier, why God doesn't remove the stones and straighten the path. If God did that, you might never get to the top, because the bumps are what you climb on."[3]

—WARREN WIERSBE

Stretcher Bearers

*A few days later, when Jesus again entered Capernaum,
the people heard that he had come home. So many gathered
that there was no room left, not even outside the door, and
he preached the word to them. Some men came, bringing
to him a paralytic, carried by four of them. Since they
could not get him to Jesus because of the crowd,
they made an opening in the roof above Jesus and,
after digging through it, lowered the mat the
paralyzed man was lying on. (Mark 2:1–4)*

On the planning team for our church's women's retreat, I had spent months praying and preparing for this momentous weekend. My heart's desire was to serve and encourage the women attending the retreat. God had a different agenda.

Friday evening, after introducing the devotional, I collapsed. Weak and in pain, I spent the remainder of the weekend in bed with yet another flare-up.

Tears trickled down my cheeks as I argued with God. *Lord, couldn't this flare-up wait until next week? Everyone else is enjoying the retreat while I'm alone.*

Judy, our house mom for the weekend, interrupted my pity party. She sacrificed her retreat activities to spend the morning with me. Judy shared the story of the paralyzed man and his friends who went to such great lengths to bring him to Jesus.

The room was packed. People had come from miles around to hear Jesus teach. The crowd was jammed so tightly together that no one could squeeze in or out. This didn't stop the paralytic's compassionate and creative friends. They climbed onto the roof, removed the tiles, and lowered their friend to Jesus.

Lying there listening to Judy, I sympathized with the paralytic. I despise feeling weak and helpless. I imagine the paralytic longed to walk into the room without assistance. How embarrassing to be lowered through the roof! Yet the paralytic needed the help of his friends. In fact, Jesus was so impressed with the faith of the paralytic's *friends* that he healed him.

Pain and weakness are selfish, demanding companions. Sometimes pain reverberates so loudly through my body that I'm unable to pray or read my Bible. As the paralytic needed his friends in order to reach Jesus, I need the friends who bring me before God in prayer. I need the strength of others when my own strength is lacking.

I learned a great deal about community while spending the retreat weekend in bed. The women surrounded me with their prayers and commitments to provide meals, housekeeping, and transportation during the coming weeks. I was amazed that by allowing them to serve me, I was serving them.

It is often difficult for those of us with chronic illness to accept help from others. We would much rather give than receive. However, we can't go it alone. God often provides his greatest strength through the ministry of our friends.

Father, thank you for the blessing of earthly friendships. Help me to graciously accept the strength you provide through others.

Two are better than one, because they have a good return for their work: If one falls down, his friend can help him up. But pity the man who falls and has no one to help him up! (Eccles. 4:9, 10)

The Furnace of Affliction

"See, I have refined you, though not as silver;
I have tested you in the furnace of affliction."

—ISAIAH 48:10

Refiner's Fire

*In this you greatly rejoice, though now for a little while
you may have had to suffer grief in all kinds of trials.
These have come so that your faith—of greater worth
than gold, which perishes even though refined by fire—
may be proved genuine and may result in praise, glory
and honor when Jesus Christ is revealed.* (1 Pet. 1:6, 7)

Lynn surveyed her ravaged body. Her red, swollen fingers refused to bend. Her nose dripped constantly, and her eyes ran rivers. The soles of Lynn's feet burned as though on fire. Her stomach churned, eager to join the rest of her body in open rebellion against this tenacious foreign invader—chemotherapy.

For months Lynn endured this fiery assault on her body. She clung to her 40 percent chance to be cured of advanced colon cancer. But some days were way too hard. "One hour! Lord, is it too much to ask to feel good for one hour?" yelled Lynn, hot tears staining her cheeks.

In 1 Peter 1:7, Paul compared the purifying of our faith with the refining of gold. Gold's refining process requires an intense amount of heat. As gold smolders in the fire, the dross—the impurities—rise to the top, and the goldsmith skims them off.

Strong and pure, the remaining gold gleams with a blinding brilliance. The goldsmith knows the refining process is complete when his own reflection stares back at him in the glow of the gold.

The crucible of illness flames with the intensity of the refiner's fire. Like other trials, pain and sickness consume the selfish, worldly scum in our lives that detracts from our relationship with the Lord. As we yield to the Lord and endure our time in the fire, we become more Christlike. Our resulting faith radiates authenticity and purity. Through our pain, people see Jesus' reflection in our lives.

The goldsmith never leaves the furnace while the gold is in the fire. Too much heat would destroy the metal. How much more precious are we than gold to God, our Refiner! Like the goldsmith, God is with us, and he carefully controls the fire. He knows just how much heat we can tolerate as he watches for the image of Jesus to shine in us.

Lynn emerged from her fiery furnace refined and reflecting Christ's glory. In remission, she serves as a Cancer Patient Advocate—ministering to the spiritual and emotional needs of cancer patients.[1]

The refiner's fire scorches. But without heat, there can be no gold. Without pain and trials, our lives won't reflect Christ as clearly. The ability to "rejoice" in our pain occurs when we keep our eyes on the end result, rather than on the painful process: the final goal—that our faith "may be proved genuine and may result in praise, glory and honor when Jesus Christ is revealed" (1 Pet. 1:7).

Father, help me to be patient and steadfast during the refining process. Leave me in the fire until my life shines with the reflection of Jesus.

He [God] will sit as a refiner and purifier. (Mal. 3:3)

God's Megaphone

"And now my life ebbs away;
days of suffering grip me. . . .
Night pierces my bones;
my gnawing pains never rest.
I cry out to you, O God, but you do not answer." (Job 30:16, 20)

"But those who suffer he [God] delivers in their suffering;
he speaks to them in their affliction." (Job 36:15)

Sharp arrows of pain stabbed my neck and shoulders. Inflamed, tender joints in my hands and knees ached. Intense weakness enveloped my body. The dreaded scenario of a simultaneous flare-up of both arthritic symptoms and fibromyalgia had struck at last.

Why did I have to endure so much pain? Surely coping with one chronic illness was enough suffering. Like Job, in my agony I cried out to God. *Where are you, Lord? Don't you care about me?* The answering silence was deafening. Had God abandoned and forsaken me? Did God abandon and forsake Job?

In her book, *Waiting for a Miracle*, Jan Markell states, "Perhaps the ultimate lesson in the Book of Job is that God's silence does *not* equate his absence."[2] God has not budged. "Silence," "wait," and "delay" are all crucial elements of God's perfect plan.

In time, God broke his silence and spoke to Job out of the whirlwind. God used a series of pointed questions and vivid illustrations drawn from nature to demonstrate that he, God, was firmly in control.

Humbled, Job came before God in reverence and awe. Although Job finally had his audience before God, he no longer needed answers. Job realized he could trust God with his unanswered questions: "I know that you can do all things; no plan of yours can be thwarted" (Job 42:2).

The tragedy and anguish God allowed in his life grabbed Job's attention and thrust him into a desperate search for his Creator. God's voice rang far louder and clearer in Job's affliction than when Job's life was free of trouble.

When my symptoms are in remission, I tend to coast in my relationship with the Lord. I seize control of my own life. It sometimes takes an illness (or two!) before God recaptures my attention.

God did not abandon Job in his affliction. Nor will he forsake us in our struggles. Our pain and distress may serve as the very instruments that amplify God's voice in our lives.

Lord, my body hurts and I feel so alone. Thank you that you are with me even when I can't feel your presence. Help me to be sensitive to the sound of your voice in my life.

"God whispers to us in our pleasures, speaks in our conscience, but shouts in our pain: it is His megaphone to rouse a deaf world."[3]

—C. S. LEWIS

Down . . . But Not Out

We are hard pressed on every side, but not crushed; perplexed,
but not in despair; persecuted, but not abandoned;
struck down, but not destroyed. (2 Cor. 4:8, 9)

Matt stepped off the plane into the blazing heat of an Israel summer. *Lord, where's my excitement and joy?* After all, this was Matt's dream military assignment. But his elation lay buried beneath the crush of overwhelming circumstances.

His brother had committed suicide six months before Matt's arrival in Israel. Miles from home, he staggered from the emotional and spiritual repercussions of his brother's death.

Like most chronic illnesses, Matt's rheumatoid disease—ankylosing spondylitis—spun out of control when he was under stress. He was a twenty-nine-year-old man wearing the body of a seventy-year-old. The painful ache in his joints screamed for attention. All of these pressures intensified against the backdrop of bombings, shootings, and the continual threat of terrorist attacks that were a part of daily life in Israel.

Paul also was squeezed in the press of severe circumstances. In his second letter to the Corinthian church, Paul recounted some of the pressures he had faced: beatings, shipwrecks, harassment, stoning, and the threat of constant danger (see 2 Cor. 11:23–28). How did Paul withstand such relentless pressure?

In the onslaught of crushing physical and emotional blows, Paul refused to be spiritually destroyed. He clung to his hope in Christ, steadfast in his belief that God would not abandon him. Each wallop drove Paul closer to Christ, allowing God's power to overcome his human weakness.

Nor did God desert Matt in his avalanche of difficulties. One day Matt stumbled across a street in a daze. The sudden screech of tires jerked him awake—one inch from the bumper of a car. God spoke to Matt in the moments following his narrow escape. The Lord reminded Matt that despite everything—the incessant waves of terror, the realities of his disease, and the grief of his brother's death—he, the God of the universe, would protect him and supply the strength he needed to endure his overwhelming pressures.

Living with chronic illness often leaves us battered and bruised. Sometimes the best we can do is just hang in there. When we persevere, refusing to surrender our hope in Christ, we may be down—but never out.

Lord, it would be so easy to collapse under the weight of my circumstances. Instead, may these pressures draw me closer to you.

"It doesn't matter, really, how great the pressure is. It only matters *where the pressure lies*. See that it never comes *between* you and the Lord—then, the greater the pressure, the more it presses you to His breast."[4]

—HUDSON TAYLOR

Pruning Shears

"I am the true vine, and my Father is the gardener. He cuts off every branch in me that bears no fruit, while every branch that does bear fruit he prunes so that it will be even more fruitful." (John 15:1, 2)

Short stubby limbs. Ragged scars. I stared at my favorite hydrangea bush and winced. Dan had sheared the lush plant until now it resembled a shriveled image of its former self.

Dan didn't intend to mutilate my hydrangea with his pruning shears. He lopped off dead, extraneous branches to enhance the quality and quantity of the leaves and flowers the bush will produce next summer. Skillful pruning is crucial for the development of healthy plants. If a plant's efforts are concentrated on growing wild, tangled branches, it has little energy left for producing fruit. Pruning also exposes a plant to vital air and sunlight.

We are similar to plants and trees when it comes to pruning. Like pruning shears, illness and pain strip us of all but the essential in our lives. With loving skill, our heavenly Father severs us from distracting entanglements in order to expose us to the light of his Son.

Pruning hurts. I flinch when God cuts off fruitful relationships and "good" activities, when poor health strips me of my ability to *do*.

The very fact that God wields his pruning shears proves I'm a vital part of his vine. In this barren state, I'm most receptive to God and his plans for developing new growth in my life.

Months pass. From the kitchen window I gaze at my hydrangea bush. Now at the height of its summer beauty, flourishing green leaves and clusters of soft blue flowers adorn the healthy plant.

Pain and sickness are sharp pruning shears. But when we submit to our Master Gardener's loving touch, the resulting fruit in our lives brings great glory to God.

Father, thank you that you hold the pruning shears in your loving hands. As I submit to painful pruning, may my life display more of your beauty.

"The shears, or knife, which cut away at the non-fruit-bearing growth are held in the hands, not of an angel, nor, for that matter, an archangel, but in the hands of our loving heavenly Father."[5]

—SELWYN HUGHES

Shattered Dreams

"For I know the plans I have for you," declares the Lord,
"plans to prosper you and not to harm you, plans
to give you hope and a future." (Jer. 29:11)

Excitement mounted as Stacey eyed her packed bags. She scanned her to-do list: the funds were raised, her visa was stamped, and the tickets were purchased. At last, after six months of preparation, Stacey was ready to board the plane to China. While there, she would lead a college student program—a dream opportunity Stacey had already turned down several times over the past five years because of lupus flare-ups. Surely God had opened the door this time.

Three days before her scheduled departure, Stacey's dream was shattered when a relapse of a virus sent her to bed. She told her coleader she would meet the team in Beijing. Stacey scrambled to glue together the broken pieces of her dream. But the relentless virus refused to release its grip on her body. Stacey ached with the disappointment of once again abandoning her ministry trip to China.

Chronic illness smashes schedules—and dreams. From an outing with a friend to a ministry opportunity in China, plans shatter as our rebellious bodies follow their own agendas.

We may reach a point where we refuse to make plans or even dare to dream. *Why bother making plans? I'll probably get sick and have to cancel them.* The sting of disappointment chips away our fragile hope.

Yet, our hope is not in *our* dreams or in *our* plans for the future, but in the Lord. He who knows the end from the beginning is in control and has a purpose far beyond what we can see with our nearsighted vision. The Lord's work in our lives is greater than our dreams.

The Lord is with us as we stand with the pieces of our crumbled dreams scattered about us. As we surrender our dreams and hopes to him, he specializes in fashioning new dreams out of broken ones, in forging something new out of the splintered pieces of our lives.

Lord, it hurts when my treasured dreams shatter. Take the smashed pieces of my hopes and plans and remold them according to your perfect plan for my life.

Many are the plans in a man's heart, but it is the LORD's purpose that prevails. (Prov. 19:21)

Partner in Suffering

Carrying his own cross, he went out to the place of
the Skull (which in Aramaic is called Golgotha).
Here they crucified him. (John 19:17, 18)

I shivered as I lay on the cold metal table. Muscle spasms rippled through my neck and shoulders as my arms were forced into position over my head. When I was situated, the doctor and technicians began the simulation procedure. For over an hour, I was measured and *tattooed* in preparation for radiation treatment for breast cancer.

Except for the needle pricks when the patient is tattooed, simulation is a relatively painless procedure. But suffering from a fibromyalgia flare-up, my neck, shoulders, and arms screamed in protest as I struggled to keep my arms over my head.

I knew I couldn't remain in this painful position another minute. Suddenly, penetrating through the clamor of pain, God brought to my mind a picture of Christ hanging on the cross. My mind's eye fastened on the agonizing position of Christ's body on the cross—especially the placement of his arms above his head. I realized he, whose suffering was beyond my comprehension, understood my discomfort as I lay on the table. I focused on this picture of Christ. The final minutes of my simulation procedure were much easier to bear.

We do not have a dispassionate Savior who is a stranger to pain. As the Son of Man, Christ experienced all manner of human afflictions. Our Lord was "pierced for our transgressions, he was crushed for our iniquities" (Isa. 53:5).

Christ already suffered each throb of our pain. He empathizes with our suffering. When no one seems to understand our aches and pains, Christ comforts us with the comfort of One who is intimately acquainted with ravaging affliction.

Since my *tattooing*, I view Christ's death on the cross with fresh eyes. Yes, that he suffered and died for my sin is of paramount importance. However, I also find tremendous encouragement in knowing my Savior identifies with my pain and shares my suffering.

> *Father, as I write this, it is Christmas Eve, and we are celebrating the birth of your Son. Thank you for sending Jesus to be both my Savior and my fellow companion on my journey through pain.*

He was despised and rejected by men, a man of sorrows, and familiar with suffering. (Isa. 53:3)

Uncomfortable
Comforters

Praise be to the God and Father of our Lord Jesus Christ,
the Father of compassion and the God of all comfort,
who comforts us in all our troubles, so that we can
comfort those in any trouble with the comfort we
ourselves have received from God. (2 Cor. 1:3, 4)

Like peering in a mirror, the words of the young woman's testimony reflected my own pain and weakness. I instantly recognized Nancy as a fellow soldier in the daily battle of living with chronic illness.

During the lunch break, Nancy and I discussed the challenges of chronic illness. Although we suffer from different diseases, we enjoyed the refreshing fellowship of sharing with someone traveling the same treacherous path. I left our time together heartened and with renewed strength.

According to John Henry Jowett, "God does not comfort us to make us comfortable, but to make us comforters."[6] As we receive encouragement from God, we have both the joy and the responsibility to turn around and channel God's comfort to a fellow sufferer.

At one time I thought I had to be completely well—comfortable—before I could encourage those in hurting places. Self-centered in my own pain, I resisted opportunities to console others who were experiencing similar difficulties.

God has taught me that I don't have to draw from some shallow well of comfort within myself in order to ease the suffering of another. He—*the God of all comfort*—supplies an abundance of comfort. He eases my own pain and allows me to come alongside someone in distress.

Those of us living with chronic illness have a unique ministry. Who better to reach out to the hurting than we who know both pain and the healing balm of God's comfort?

Father, thank you that my own suffering equips me to comfort others in pain. May I welcome opportunities to channel your comfort to someone in need.

"Our Father is preparing us to meet the deep inner needs of others by bringing us through the dark places first."[7]

—CHARLES R. SWINDOLL

Through Deep Waters

"He reached down from on high and took hold of me;

he drew me out of deep waters."

—2 SAMUEL 22:17

Stormy Weather

*A furious squall came up, and the waves broke over the
boat, so that it was nearly swamped. Jesus was in the stern,
sleeping on a cushion. The disciples woke him and said to
him, "Teacher, don't you care if we drown?" He got up,
rebuked the wind and said to the waves, "Quiet! Be still!"
Then the wind died down and it was completely calm.
He said to his disciples, "Why are you so afraid?
Do you still have no faith?"* (Mark 4:37–40)

The wind roared in my ears. Each surging wave tossed the
sailboat with reckless abandon. My hands gripped the side
of the boat.

Ten years old, I was alone with my dad in a small sailboat on
Lake Tahoe. As black storm clouds formed overhead, the placid,
friendly lake suddenly turned into an angry, churning sea.

Terrified, I looked up at my dad. He must have been in a
state of panic himself as he fought to control the boat. Yet my
childish faith in my father's ability to bring us safely to shore
calmed the worst of my fears.

When the storms of illness buffet my life, I once again become that ten-year-old girl caught in a storm on Lake Tahoe. Gusts of pain threaten to drown me. The fear of becoming an invalid chokes me. My body and emotions are whipped about by the assault of poor health.

During these recurring squalls of illness, I remember how I trusted my earthly father to keep control and guide our boat through the storm. How much more can I trust my heavenly Father to carry me through stormy times of pain and weakness.

In turbulent times of illness, we can understand the fear, panic, and yes, even the lack of faith of the disciples caught in the violent storm. Like the disciples, we need to look to Jesus, our anchor and guide through the tempestuous waters of illness.

Father, when the storms of sickness rage through me, quell the waves of pain and panic in my heart.

He stilled the storm to a whisper; the waves of the sea were hushed. They were glad when it grew calm, and he guided them to their desired haven. (Ps. 107:29, 30)

Deep Waters

"When you pass through the waters,
I will be with you;
and when you pass through the rivers,
they will not sweep over you." (Isa. 43:2)

With unseeing eyes, I flipped through the pages of a magazine. Tossing it back onto the table, I glanced around the clinic's waiting room. *Were all these people as anxious and fidgety as I?*

New symptoms had driven me back to the doctor's office. Severe muscle spasms in my neck and shoulders now joined my collection of bodily complaints.

Although painful, these muscular warning signs did not prepare me for the doctor's words: "You have fibromyalgia." Relief that I now had a name for my symptoms crashed against the dread of coping with a second chronic disease. Already overwhelmed with physical maladies, this new disease threatened to drown me.

In Isaiah 43:2, God does not promise to be with us *if* we face difficulties. He promises his presence *when* we encounter troubled waters. Hard times are inevitable in this life. But God is right there in the surging river with us.

In addition, God does not leave us floundering in the water. In the introduction to her book *Help Lord, I'm Sinking*, Carole Mayhall states, "God says *'through the waters'* which means *there is another side*."[1] Not only do we have God's promise of his presence, but he will also deliver us to the other side of our difficulties.

God has brought me through many rivers of flare-ups and infections since I was diagnosed with fibromyalgia. If I cling to him, I will not drown—no matter how rough the current.

Lord, thank you that you are with me in the midst of life's troubled waters. May I trust you to bring me safely to the other side.

"I don't have to live in fear of the storms, whether a tidal wave threatens or many smaller waves constantly rock me. Christ is in control of everything—all the circumstances in my life—and He is also the Captain of my boat."[2]

—CAROLE MAYHALL

Don't Look Down!

*Then Peter got down out of the boat, walked on the
water and came toward Jesus. But when he saw the wind,
he was afraid and, beginning to sink, cried out,
"Lord, save me!"* (Matt. 14:29, 30)

Would summer ever end? I lay in bed, my mind glued
on the turbulent events of the last few months.

My mom was battling cancer. Our newly hired
children's librarians were unable to begin their jobs until
September. I, who struggled to fulfill my own job responsibilities, now assumed the work of three librarians. I was deluged
with the numerous tasks involved in arranging the children's
area of a new branch library.

My body protested the extra activities and stress. Fatigue,
muscle pain, and throat infections battered my body. Focused
on overwhelming demands, I was sinking in a sea of challenging circumstances.

Peter also exhibited tunnel vision. With great excitement,
he climbed out of the boat and started toward Jesus. But then,

distracted by the wind, Peter took his eyes off Jesus and fixed them on the pounding waves crashing around him. He started to sink.

Floundering in the water, Peter cried out to the Lord. "Immediately Jesus reached out his hand and caught him" (Matt. 14:31). Peter looked up and refocused his attention on Christ. With the Lord's help, he climbed back into the boat.

It is easy to become engulfed by chronic illness. Discomfort, weakness, and treatments threaten to submerge us. The daily demands of illness absorb most of our energy and attention. We're unable to see above our pain.

Like Peter, we need to fix our eyes on the Lord. Time spent reading the Bible and talking with the Lord in prayer helps us focus on him.

The churning waves of circumstances and tasks did not die down that summer. But as I fastened my eyes on the Lord, he carried me through each turbulent day.

Lord, when I develop tunnel vision and can't see beyond the swells of pain, help me to focus my eyes on you.

"When the storms of life come down upon you, keep your eyes fixed on Jesus."[3]

—GEORGE SWEETING

Refuge in the Storm

In you, O LORD, I have taken refuge;
let me never be put to shame;
deliver me in your righteousness.
Turn your ear to me,
come quickly to my rescue;
be my rock of refuge,
a strong fortress to save me. (Ps. 31:1, 2)

Cheryl dragged herself down the aisles of the store, oblivious to the sea of people swirling around her. Her need for groceries clashed with her desire to go home and rest. She'd already exhausted her limited supply of energy taking her son to the orthodontist.

Each time she reached for an item on the grocery shelves, Cheryl's body protested.

At last Cheryl staggered to the checkout line. Her hands gripped the grocery cart as she waited for her turn. *Can't this line move any faster?* A sudden wave of weakness swept over her. Feeling lightheaded, Cheryl started to faint. Someone guided her to a nearby bench.

It seemed as though all eyes in the store were focused on her. Drenched with embarrassment, Cheryl longed to run and hide from the curious onlookers. When the weakness finally passed, Cheryl edged out to her car, and her son drove her home.

Arriving home, Cheryl sought refuge in her bedroom. A physical and emotional storm raged within her as she replayed the scene in the grocery store. She cried out to God. *Lord, I feel so vulnerable! Why does my body fail me? Help me, Lord! Please help me!*

In Psalm 31, David uttered a similar cry for help. Hounded by those in constant pursuit of him, a beaten and bruised David fled to God—his one true Refuge, Fortress, and Deliverer. God was David's shelter: the place where he could bind his wounds and receive renewed strength for the battle.

Behind her closed bedroom door, Cheryl hid in the shelter of God. Regardless of the embarrassing circumstances and the physical assault on her body, God would sustain and restore her. He was her source of hope.

The storms of illness gust into our lives, leaving us hurt and exposed. Sometimes we need to withdraw and regroup. When the tempest blusters loudest, we can run, walk, or crawl to God. We emerge from his fortress strengthened and ready to face the battle again.

Father, thank you that you are my refuge and strength. When physical and emotional storms buffet me, you alone are my stronghold.

"The eternal God is your refuge, and underneath are the everlasting arms." (Deut. 33:27)

A Firm Foundation

*"The rain came down, the streams rose, and the winds
blew and beat against that house; yet it did not fall,
because it had its foundation on the rock."* (Matt. 7:25)

Heavy rains. Swollen rivers. Mudslides. December often
ushers in flood season in western Washington. Each
year, homes in low-lying areas collapse under the
weight of water and mud.

The daily pressures of illness lead to similar flooding. The
torrent of constant pain, fatigue, and the side effects of medication can erode my spiritual as well as my physical "house."
Doubt and fear seep in, threatening the very fabric of my relationship with the Lord. How can my "spiritual house" survive
when rivers of illness reach flood stage?

When illness engulfs my life, Christ the Rock must be my
foundation. Otherwise, I sink into the mire of self-pity and
despair. Like the foolish man who built his house upon the sand
(Matt. 7:26, 27), if I construct my spiritual house on any foundation other than Christ, the result is destruction.

We gird our foundation in Christ by spending time in his Word, praying, and as we worship and fellowship with him. Our ability to withstand the onslaught of chronic disease is proportional to the strength of our relationship with Christ.

We must not wait until our illness reaches flood stage before we lay our foundation in Christ. The time to secure the house is before the flood. We need to build our relationship with the Lord on a daily basis.

When rivers of sickness crest, we can rejoice because Christ is the bedrock of our spiritual foundation.

Lord, you are the cornerstone of my life. Thank you that when rivers of illness threaten to overwhelm me, I can stand firm in you.

For no one can lay any foundation other than the one already laid, which is Jesus Christ. (1 Cor. 3:11)

The Calm in the Storm

You will keep in perfect peace
him whose mind is steadfast,
because he trusts in you. (Isa. 26:3)

Karen dragged herself to her car and slumped across the steering wheel. Arrows of pain targeted her neck and shoulders. Numb with exhaustion, she turned on the ignition and drove back to her realtor's office.

Swells of anger, frustration, and despair swept over her. *How can I negotiate the best deals for my clients? This horrible pain and fatigue is so distracting! I'm failing at the job I love.*

Stress and pressure exacerbated Karen's fibromyalgia symptoms. Soon she was caught in the turmoil of deciding whether or not to even continue her career as a real estate agent. She was the major provider for her family—her income was important. But how much longer could she push herself to continue?

After months of agonizing over her decision, Karen finally quit her job. Soon her family was caught in a whirlwind of drastic lifestyle changes. They lost their home with its beautiful gardens. Karen and her husband replaced their cars with older models. No longer the major contributor to her family's finances, Karen faced an enormous emotional adjustment. She mourned for the job that had brought her such satisfaction.

Like Karen, many of us are tossed into turbulent waters because of health issues. Each day brings painful challenges. Illness agitates every area of our lives. How can we find peace amid the storm raging within us?

Isaiah 26:3 offers us the one true prescription for peace. This inner peace has nothing to do with our circumstances. We can't create it on our own. True peace is found in God: "The LORD is Peace" (Judg. 6:24). We appropriate this peace by fixing our minds on the Lord—by keeping our thoughts on him and trusting him, regardless of the problems surging about us.

Karen learned that peace isn't the absence of difficulties. But an inexplicable calm swept over her as she fastened her mind on the Lord and relinquished control of her circumstances to him. Trusting God enough to let go of her situation paved the way for the peace she now enjoys. Now Karen doesn't miss her old job—not even for a minute.

Life with an illness consists of one deluge after another. But as we fix our eyes on the Lord, he will provide a cushion of calm in the center of every storm.

Lord, as the storms of illness rage about me, help me to find perfect peace in you.

"For he himself is our peace." (Eph. 2:14)

Courage in the Darkness

The LORD is my light and my salvation—
whom shall I fear?
The LORD is the stronghold of my life—
of whom shall I be afraid?

—PSALM 27:1

Trusting God in the Dark

Who among you fears the LORD
and obeys the word of his servant?
Let him who walks in the dark,
who has no light,
trust in the name of the LORD
and rely on his God. (Isa. 50:10)

With leaden feet and a weary body, Marilyn mustered the energy to take a walk in the warm autumn breeze. She gazed at the golden leaves shimmering in the blaze of the afternoon sun and wondered why her heart was so cold to the beauty around her. Where radiant hope had once dwelled, only darkness remained. Fatigue and depression had extinguished any light in her heart. Trudging through the meadow, Marilyn cried out to her heavenly Father, who seemed absent from her life. *God, why does it have to be this dark?*

Fear of the unknown often grips our hearts. It is one of our deepest fears. As humans, we cherish control, and we panic when we can't see more than a step ahead of us.

It requires faith to entrust the unknown to God. In Hebrews 11, we encounter the "Hall of Faith." Here we read the accounts of men and women who died without seeing the fulfillment of God's promises for them—Noah, Abraham, Rahab, among others. Even so, they never faltered in their belief that God would accomplish his purposes. Their ability to trust God in the dark shines through the ages as an example to us.

No shout from heaven or audible voice reached Marilyn's ears in response to her cry. Instead, God penetrated the darkness and deadness of her heart with questions of his own: *Will you trust me in the dark when there is no glimmer of light? Will you trust me in the "not yet," this time on earth when all that I've promised you is not yet experienced?*

Although the darkness and pain remained, Marilyn's view of God shifted. She realized how much her desire for control kept her from truly trusting him. Marilyn relinquished her demand that God be predictable—and controllable. Her prayer for an end to the blackness in her soul changed to: *I will trust you, Lord, to shine in my darkness in your way and in your time.*

A flashlight only illuminates a minute section of the path at a time. But this small circle of light is all we really need. With each succeeding step, the glow of the flashlight moves farther along the path, guiding us to the end of our journey.

God sheds a similar flashlight-sized beam of light on the thick darkness of our circumstances. We squint through the blackness of pain, barely able to see the next ray of light. But no matter how bleak our situation, we can always rely on the light of God's presence. For we walk "by faith, not by sight" (2 Cor. 5:7).

Father, at times, this journey of illness seems dark and terrifying. When I can't see beyond the blackness of my circumstances, help me to walk in the light of your presence.

"The message of darkness is to teach us to lean on God."[1]

—JAN COLEMAN

A Roller Coaster Ride

And He shall be the stability of your times. (Isa. 33:6 NASB)

C ome on, Aunt Judy," begged Allie. "It's just a baby roller coaster. You can do it."

My hands and legs trembled as I climbed into a car on this "baby" roller coaster and sat down next to my niece. With a loud "clack-clack," our car lurched to the top of the first hill.

I clamped my eyes shut and clung to the safety bar. Our car plunged to the bottom and then rocketed up the next incline. Surely I'd left my stomach at the bottom of the last hill.

Life with a chronic illness often mimics a roller coaster ride. Symptoms of diseases such as lupus and fibromyalgia are cyclical in nature. One day we may feel great, exploding with energy. The next day, stricken with a flare-up, we descend to the depths of pain and fatigue.

This unpredictability disturbs my structured, orderly nature. Coping with symptoms today is far easier for me than not knowing how I will feel tomorrow. "Good" days are spoiled as I fret about how long they will last. Making plans becomes a distasteful guessing game. How do I respond when someone says, "But you were fine yesterday"?

As Christians, we have the privilege of gripping something far more secure than a metal safety bar as we ride this roller coaster of volatile symptoms: the faithfulness of God. Jesus is as constant and unwavering today as he was yesterday and will be tomorrow. He is with us in the downward spirals as well as on the heights of our "good" days.

The roller coaster of chronic disease makes steep drops and corkscrew turns. Yet we trust in the living God who knows what is lurking around the next curve.

Lord, thank you that you are the one constant in my life. In spite of my fickle health, may I live in today, trusting you for tomorrow.

"Jesus Christ is the same yesterday and today and forever." (Heb. 13:8)

What If?

*"So do not fear, for I am with you;
do not be dismayed, for I am your God.
I will strengthen you and help you;
I will uphold you with my righteous right hand." (Isa. 41:10)*

Stacey took a deep breath as apprehension mingled with excitement. Attending graduate school was a major commitment. Before the ink had even dried on the registration forms, Stacey was struck with a severe attack of the "what ifs"—potentially more destructive than her chronic illness.

What if I'm not well enough when the program begins in January? I was housebound with illness most of last winter. What if my body refuses to meet the demands of a busy class schedule? What if physical weakness and unpredictable symptoms force me to withdraw from the program? Riddled with fear, Stacey's vivid imagination fueled additional stress on her already weakened body.

We are especially susceptible to fear in the center of illness. "What ifs" thrive in the fertile soil of our exhausted bodies and emotions. Before long we are incarcerated in the prison of our own fears.

The chief antidote to the "what ifs" and their resulting fear lies in recognizing that God is not the author of fear. In his second letter to Timothy, Paul declared, "For God did not give us a spirit of timidity, but a spirit of power, of love and of self-discipline" (2 Tim. 1:7).

Throughout the Bible, God commands us to "fear not." In his book, *You Gotta Keep Dancin'*, Tim Hansel notes that there are 365 "fear nots" in the Bible. "Could it be that it is to remind us *daily* that we need not fear the difficulties that all of us eventually have to face?"[2]

The words *fear not* encourage us to trust in God. He promises to be with us no matter how dark and frightening the situation. He will illuminate the road before us with the light of his presence.

When illness strikes, we don't have to succumb to the "what ifs." Our hope and confidence is in God, whose "perfect love drives out fear" (1 John 4:18).

> *Father, thank you that I don't have to be a prisoner of my fears. When the "what ifs" attack, may I be quick to run to you.*

I sought the LORD, and he answered me; he delivered me from all my fears. (Ps. 34:4)

Encounter with a Giant

*"The L*ORD *who delivered me from the paw of the lion
and the paw of the bear will deliver me from the
hand of this Philistine." (1 Sam. 17:37)*

Barely breathing, I froze as sharp flashes of pain stabbed my chest. *Oh, no, Lord,* I prayed as the pain eased. *Please don't let something* else *be wrong with me!*

I dreaded the prospect of more tests, especially if they showed that yet another system of my body was malfunctioning. Fear, more intense than the chest pains, squeezed my heart.

After a few more weeks of sporadic chest pains, I dragged myself to the doctor. Initial tests indicated a heart blockage. Now my *giant* had a name: heart disease. Shock mingled with fear. I drove home in a daze.

The next hurdle was a cardiac catheterization. The night before the procedure, sleep deserted me. Switching on the lamp, I opened my Bible to 1 Samuel.

In 1 Samuel 17, David was approaching his battle with Goliath. Deep within, David must have trembled in anticipation of his encounter with the daunting giant.

Through his fear, David recalled how, while tending sheep, God had rescued him from both the lion and the bear. David trusted this same God to deliver him from Goliath. At the conclusion of verse 37, Saul said to David, "Go, and the LORD be with you."

Like David, the Lord is with me in my battles. As I finally turned out the light that night, my mind flooded with memories of the times when God had delivered me—the evening he enabled me to present a workshop in spite of a debilitating fibromyalgia flare-up, and the comfort of God's presence as I lay on the table during radiation treatments for breast cancer.

By the end of 1 Samuel 17, David, empowered by God, had defeated Goliath. And soon David would rely on God's strength as he confronted new challenges. I'm sure his memory of God's deliverance over Goliath encouraged David each time he faced these new battles.

Pain clouds our memories. The current giant consumes our attention. Yet when we replay God's provision in the past, we realize that God will deliver us from these new giants. Even heart disease.

> *Thank you, Lord, for the gift of memory. As I face future Goliaths, may I be encouraged by the memories of how you have delivered me in the past.*

"He who has been with us in six troubles will not forsake us in the seventh."[3]

—CHARLES SPURGEON

The Waiting Game

Wait for the LORD;
be strong and take heart
and wait for the LORD. (Ps. 27:14)

I stared at the telephone, willing it to ring. *Dr. Blake must have the test results by now. Why doesn't he call me? My* stomach churned with impatience.

In this world of megabytes and instant everything, those of us with chronic illness become reluctant pros at playing the waiting game. We spend an inordinate amount of time in doctors' aptly named "waiting rooms." Time drags while we languish in bed waiting for medications or treatments to take effect. We cling to shreds of hope as we wait for researchers to discover cures for our illnesses.

Throughout the Bible, we find role models of proficient "waiters." It was almost eight months from the time Noah's ark rested on Ararat until Noah, his family, and the animals stepped out on dry land. Abraham was 100 years of age when Sarah gave birth to Isaac. Before becoming king, David spent fourteen years fleeing from Saul.

As each of these biblical figures learned, we exercise our muscles of faith in God's waiting room. Our patience and trust in God are stretched when we experience delays. Faith and hope develop as we learn to entrust life's interruptions to God.

I find it easier to cope with waiting periods when I remember that God operates according to his own perfect timetable. He who sees the end from the beginning is never late or in a hurry.

Learning to play the waiting game is difficult. We fuss and chomp at the bit. But as Psalm 27:14 encourages us, we can "take heart" because we are waiting "for the LORD." He will always be right on time.

Lord, forgive me for the times when I'm impatient and demand immediate answers. Help me to make wise use of the time I spend in your waiting room.

"We shall not grow weary of waiting upon God if we remember how long and how graciously He once waited for us."[4]

—CHARLES SPURGEON

Lighting the Darkness

When Jesus spoke again to the people, he said, "I am the light of the world. Whoever follows me will never walk in darkness, but will have the light of life." (John 8:12)

Strapped to the moving table, Bill watched as he inched headfirst through the slender opening of the MRI tube. His eyes caught the narrowing of the tube's opening. Suffocating fear gripped him. Panic set in. *I can't breathe! Let me out! Let me out!*

His heart pounding, Bill squeezed the rubber ball placed in his hand for just such emergencies. The attendants quickly reversed the table and rolled him out of the tube and into the lighted room.

Shaken, Bill faced two equally distasteful alternatives. He could return home (a three-hour drive), ask his doctor to order a sedative, and try the MRI another day. Or Bill could immediately reenter the cramped, dark MRI tube.

Numerous black tunnels of fear litter the landscape of illness: the dread of growing limitations and continued pain, qualms about medical tests and the results of these tests, and the anxiety of possible relapses. We grope in the frightening darkness of pain and an uncertain future.

We are not alone in the deepest of these pitch-black caves. God, who created both light and darkness, pushes back our darkest fears with the shining light of his presence. He is right there with us! As we follow Jesus, the Light of the world, the Lord illuminates the path before us.

Bill knew that scheduling a new appointment could take months. He didn't want to waste more time and money. Bill agreed to enter the MRI tube again—this time with his eyes closed and his heart fixed on the Lord. The radiance of God's presence penetrated the coal black tube. Songs and choruses filled Bill's mind. He praised and worshipped God to the accompaniment of the MRI magnets thundering inside the tube as they created images of his spine.

The confines of an MRI tube. The terror of a cancer diagnosis. The dread of continuing pain and weakness. It is in the darkest places of our lives that God's light shines the brightest.

Lord, thank you that no darkness is so black that it can snuff out the light of your presence.

"There is no darkness so great that Jesus cannot dispel it."[5]

—CORRIE TEN BOOM

Treasures of Darkness

"I will give you the treasures of darkness,
riches stored in secret places,
so that you may know that I am the LORD,
the God of Israel, who summons you by name." (Isa. 45:3)

The shadows cast over my life grew darker with each passing day. Within a five-month period, I was hospitalized three times for clinical depression, diagnosed with breast cancer, and lost my mother to cancer. In addition, radiation treatments for breast cancer were exacerbating the symptoms of my chronic illness.

Each succeeding blow thrust me deeper into an endless, dark tunnel of grief and despair. The encircling blackness seemed to snuff out the light of God's presence. For months, I groped alone in the dark. *Where was God? Would this darkness ever end?*

One day while floundering through my devotional time, I stumbled across the words of Isaiah 45:3. Stunned, I read the verse a second time. *Treasures? Riches?* God would bring something of value out of this bleak time in my life? A glimmer of light and hope penetrated the darkness.

The darkness did not lift overnight. God chose to keep these treasures in "secret places" for a time. Meanwhile I experienced new lessons in endurance and trust—lessons best learned in the dark.

The darkness hovering over me finally began to dissipate. At last I was ready to receive the treasures God had mined in my black tunnel of despair. I realized anew the value of my relationship with the Lord. My trust in God grew as he guided me through the most devastating time of my life.

In the last month before her death, my mother and I drew closer as we fought cancer. A compassion for those suffering emotional pain evolved out of my struggle with depression. Coping with breast cancer forced me to develop good diet and exercise habits that benefited my overall health. What riches God brought out of my darkest hour!

I have a plaque on my bookshelf that reads: WE CAN ONLY APPRECIATE THE MIRACLE OF A SUNRISE IF WE HAVE WAITED IN DARKNESS. Chronic illness often resembles a dark continuous tunnel. At times, we despair of ever seeing light again. We wait for the sunrise.

In God's time, he will lead us out of the darkness into the light of his Son. And God's *treasures* in *secret places* will be invaluable because they were quarried in the darkness of pain.

Father, thank you for the treasures you have cultivated in my darkest hour. Help me to keep my eyes focused on your light at the end of my tunnel of pain.

But you are a chosen people, a royal priesthood, a holy nation, a people belonging to God, that you may declare the praises of him who called you out of darkness into his wonderful light. (1 Pet. 2:9)

Springs in the Desert

"I am making a way in the desert
and streams in the wasteland."

—ISAIAH 43:19

Desert Places

*"I will lead her into the desert
and speak tenderly to her."* (Hosea 2:14)

At once the Spirit sent him out into the desert. (Mark 1:12)

Barren hills. Shimmering waves of heat. Smatterings of scrub brush. Tantalizing snow-capped mountains in the far-off distance. Looking out the car window, my hot, blurry eyes scanned the sun-scorched landscape of the Mojave Desert. Tired and impatient, I longed to put the desert behind me and bask in the refreshment of the Sierra Nevada Mountains.

Relentless stretches of chronic illness can be as stark of a wasteland as the sweltering Mojave Desert. Torrid pain saps our parched bodies and spirits. Waves of weakness sweep over us like windblown sand. We despair of ever feeling well again. How we'd love to avoid desert experiences!

Throughout the Bible, God called his people to the desert. The character of the Israelites was tested and molded for forty years under the blazing desert sun. David learned to depend on God while hiding in the wilderness. For forty days Jesus withstood Satan's temptations in the desert.

Like the men and women in the Bible, we draw closest to God in the desert places of our lives. Stripped of distractions, we hear God's message more clearly in the stillness of the desert.

The desert experiences in our lives are not desolate wastelands. As we learn to trust God in the scorching heat of chronic pain and illness, our faith flourishes with the tenacity of a desert wildflower. In our Father's guiding hand, the deserts we travel across become fertile ground for spiritual growth and blessing. We prefer to dwell on lush mountain peaks. Yet when God tenderly calls us to the flat, arid desert, he may be doing his richest work in our lives.

> *Lord, thank you for the bleak and barren times you allow in my life. May my faith grow as I spend time with you in the desert.*

"Stars shine brighter in the desert. There are no obstructions, no distractions, no competing lights. The view from the valley isn't so bad because Jesus shines so clearly."[1]

—JOHN WIMBER

The Desert of Loneliness

Turn to me and be gracious to me,
for I am lonely and afflicted. (Ps. 25:16)

"Yet I am not alone, for my Father is with me." (John 16:32)

Alone on the island of my bed, I tossed from side to side. *Why doesn't someone call to ask how I'm feeling? Didn't anyone miss me at church this morning?* The ache of loneliness was more intense than the pain of my throbbing muscles.

As a single woman, I've adjusted to the unique challenges of living alone. But when illness strikes, my independent spirit quavers in the face of pain and weakness. *Why do I have to confront this disease alone?* The vacuum of loneliness consumes my being.

Loneliness can be an insidious offshoot of chronic illness. We require large doses of quiet and solitude in order to regain our strength. We can feel detached from well-meaning family and friends who don't understand our illnesses.

Jesus journeyed across this desert of loneliness. His dearest friends abandoned him in the Garden of Gethsemane. On the cross, Jesus cried out, "My God, my God, why have you forsaken me?" (Matt. 27:46), as he suffered the ultimate loneliness—separation from God.

During his ministry on earth, Jesus didn't shirk away from lonely desert experiences. He knew the value of spending time alone with God and often withdrew to "lonely places." These times of solitude with God strengthened and prepared Jesus for the rigors of his ministry on earth.

Many times I fail to perceive loneliness as a gift rather than a curse. It is in my secluded lonely places that I draw close to God and he accomplishes his richest work in me.

The silent confinement of our bedrooms screams in our ears. The phone doesn't ring. The mailbox is empty. We feel abandoned by those closest to us. However, time spent in this arid desert of loneliness is time to remember that we are never truly alone. Jesus, our constant companion, walks with us. He, who most understands our loneliness, refreshes us with his eternal presence.

Lord, thank you for the promise of your everlasting presence with me. Help me to use my lonely places as opportunities to deepen my relationship with you.

"To live a spiritual life, we must first find the courage to enter into the desert of loneliness and to change it by gentle and persistent efforts into the garden of solitude."[2]

—HENRI NOUWEN

Gaining through Loss

What is more, I consider everything a loss compared to the surpassing greatness of knowing Christ Jesus my Lord, for whose sake I have lost all things. I consider them rubbish, that I may gain Christ and be found in him. (Phil. 3:8, 9)

To the casual observer, Brenda had it all: a loving family, a beautiful home, and a dream job. But excruciating chronic pain smoldered beneath the surface, threatening to consume all that Brenda held dear.

For years Brenda fluctuated between trying to ignore the pain and willing it away. But the tenacious pain screamed for attention. One morning Brenda could no longer snub it. She dressed gingerly and drove to work where she collapsed, unable to move.

In the following weeks, debilitating pain destroyed cherished pieces of Brenda's life. She gave up her job. Because she could no longer climb stairs, her family was forced to sell their beloved home. No longer able to drive, Brenda surrendered her car keys.

Intense pain robbed her of the joy of participating in the planning and preparations for her daughter's wedding. She attended her daughter's wedding in a pain-induced daze—unable to remember details of the joyous event. Friends grew weary of her illness and drifted away. Despite the support of her husband and children, Brenda's illness slowly unraveled her life, layer by layer.

Chronic illness amputates much from our lives including our health, independence, jobs, favorite activities, and friends. We encounter severe lifestyle changes, while at the same time, our dreams for the future are dashed.

The apostle Paul understood the pain of loss. He possessed superb credentials and was a man of outstanding accomplishments. He also faced tremendous loss. Yet, Paul counted his achievements as garbage compared to his priceless relationship with Christ. When all was stripped away, Paul still retained his intimacy with Christ.

When illness slashes through our lives, we need to take time to grieve our losses. Then, like Paul, we can find joy in what we've gained in the midst of our loss—our growing knowledge of and relationship with our Lord, Jesus Christ.

Looking back, Brenda's greatest gain was the knowledge that God's grace is sufficient in every pain and loss. Although God hasn't healed her physically, he's healed her in a spiritual sense—which is much more important than any physical mending. Brenda says she wouldn't trade her deepening relationship with Christ for anything—even her car keys.

Thank you, Lord, that in spite of all I've lost, I've gained a deeper, more intimate relationship with you.

"As we live each day with the memory of our old lives, we do not have to be sad or confused about who we are now. We can live with the losses and realize that if they propel us to Christ, then we have gained a great deal more than we have lost."[3]

—CHRISTINA SMITH

Sacrifice of Praise

*Though the fig tree does not bud
and there are no grapes on the vines,
though the olive crop fails
and the fields produce no food,
though there are no sheep in the pen
and no cattle in the stalls,
yet I will rejoice in the LORD,
I will be joyful in God my Savior.* (Hab. 3:17, 18)

*L*ord, we lift your name on high. Lord, we love to sing your praises." I stood with the rest of the congregation but only mouthed the words of the chorus. The word *praises* stuck in my throat.

Pain gnawed my arms and legs. My swollen fingers resembled sausages rather than normal appendages. Exhausted, I felt detached from the rest of the worshipers. Instead of sweet praises, bitter anger and resentment bubbled out of my heart.

Praise effuses out of our hearts when symptoms of illness are in remission. But it requires grit and sheer determination to praise God in the midst of pain. This is when we truly understand what the writer of Hebrews called "a sacrifice of praise"

(Heb. 13:15): choosing to praise God when everything within us screams otherwise.

By its very name, this sacrifice of praise costs us something. We must lay aside our anger, fears, and yes, even our desire to be well.

Abraham demonstrated this "sacrifice of praise" when he laid Isaac, his son, on the altar. Throughout the Psalms, David exalted God in the center of devastating conditions.

It's crucial to remember that we are offering our praise because of who God is—not because of our circumstances. This praise is not born of resignation, but is presented as a gift to God.

My difficulties don't happen to include barren fig trees and failed crops. However, though my hands ache and weakness rules my body, though limitations abound and apprehension overcomes me, "yet I will rejoice in the LORD, I will be joyful in God my Savior."

Lord, in the midst of pain and weakness, I choose to lift my voice in praise to you. May my sacrifice of praise bring glory and honor to your name.

"I think that God is especially honored when we offer a sacrifice of praise. He is glorified when we offer words of adoration wrenched from a pained and bruised heart. Perhaps that's because He values the precious weight of each word of praise that's been sacrificed."[4]

—JONI EARECKSON TADA, *GLORIOUS INTRUDER*

Oasis in the Desert

As the deer pants for streams of water,
so my soul pants for you, O God. (Ps. 42:1)

O God, you are my God,
earnestly I seek you;
my soul thirsts for you,
my body longs for you,
in a dry and weary land
where there is no water. (Ps. 63:1)

Wads of cotton seem to line my mouth. I rub my thick tongue over parched and peeling lips. The nasty dry-mouth side effect of medication leaves me craving a glass of cool water.

Too often, I experience a similar dry-mouth syndrome in my spiritual life. Sapped by pain and the daily realities of poor health, my relationship with Christ becomes arid and distant. The result is a spiritual drought. Prayer and Bible reading wither into rote exercises. I become a dreary desert of misery and defeat.

In Psalm 63, David recognized his own spiritual thirst. He had been driven from home by the followers of his rebellious son, Absalom. David fled to the desert. Desolate, he cried out to God. In a barren wasteland, David knew that only God could quench his thirsty soul: "My soul will be satisfied as with the richest of foods; with singing lips my mouth will praise you" (Ps. 63:5).

Like David, God is our oasis in the parched deserts of illness and spiritual dryness. His invigorating springs take many forms. As we cry out to him, God's enduring presence comforts and refreshes us. His Word replenishes our weary souls. The words of a hymn or praise song soothe troubled emotions. Our prayers water the withered gardens of our spirits.

Like water quenches a thirsty body, so God's Word refreshes our dehydrated souls.

Lord, during times of spiritual drought, may I thirst for you with the intensity of David. Thank you for refreshing me with your presence and replenishing me through your Word.

"The wild animals honor me, the jackals and the owls, because I provide water in the desert and streams in the wasteland, to give drink to my people, my chosen." (Isa. 43:20)

The Good Old Days

For I have learned to be content whatever the circumstances.
I know what it is to be in need, and I know what it is
to have plenty. I have learned the secret of being content
in any and every situation, whether well fed or hungry,
whether living in plenty or in want. (Phil. 4:11, 12)

Rick and Anna stood at the altar, surrounded by family and friends. As they exchanged marriage vows, their future seemed as bright as the candlelight illuminating the sanctuary.

Two years later, the onset of Anna's troubling physical symptoms cast a shadow over their plans. Assaulted by muscular pain, most days, Anna's energy reserves wavered between low and empty. Although the diagnosis of chronic fatigue syndrome and fibromyalgia gave a name to her symptoms, Anna's fragile health encroached on the life she and Rick had envisioned.

Soon, Anna yearned for the "good old days." She craved the limitless energy she'd enjoyed only a few years earlier. Anna's mind churned. *I wish Rick had known the younger, healthier Anna.*

The apostle Paul was familiar with the "good old days" syndrome. Surely in the midst of beatings, shipwrecks, hunger, thirst, and imprisonment, Paul indulged in moments of discontent. Contentment wasn't an automatic response for Paul—something he could muster up for himself.

In Philippians 4:11, Paul stated that he "learned to be content" through the experiences God allowed in his life. Bombarded with difficulties, he realized that circumstances do not define contentment. Paul's secret for true contentment of the heart was found in his relationship with Christ. In Christ, Paul found the strength to accept and meet the challenges of each situation. Regardless of the circumstances, for Paul, Christ was enough.

The Lord taught Anna lessons in contentment, too. The words of her favorite Scripture verse, "Trust in the LORD with all your heart" (Prov. 3:5, 6), gave Anna the courage to embrace the reality of her "now." As she trusted in the Lord, she gained a new appreciation for all she and Rick possessed in Christ. A thankful heart and trust in the Lord's sufficiency replaced dwelling on her life before the illness.

Unfilled longings are scattered across this imperfect, earthly life. Living with illness is a harsh reality. But as we find our sufficiency in Christ and not in our circumstances, we will experience true contentment. Contentment far richer than we had in the "good old days."

Lord, thank you that you are sufficient for every need. Sick or well, may I, like Paul, find contentment in you.

"*Godliness with contentment is great gain.*" (1 Tim. 6:6)

The Laugh Box

A cheerful heart is good medicine,
but a crushed spirit dries up the bones. (Prov. 17:22)

She is clothed with strength and dignity;
she can laugh at the days to come. (Prov. 31:25)

I pushed the button on the top of the small plastic box. Immediately, shrieks of laughter bellowed out of the box and swirled around the classroom.

This canned laughter was the only humor I could manufacture during my school visits to promote the library's summer reading program. Muscle pain, exhaustion, and severe depression had drained my reservoir of joy. Ironically, the theme for our summer reading program was "Laugh It Up!" How I relied on the artificial guffaws of the laugh box as I encouraged students to join "Laugh It Up!"

Laughter is a powerful antitoxin in our battle against chronic disease. It is a scientific fact that the physical act of laughing releases endorphins, pain-inhibiting chemicals, in the brain. Studies show that laughter also strengthens the body's immune system.

Yet, who feels like chuckling at endless aches and pains? Where is the humor in debilitating disease? The weight of our circumstances smothers joy and laughter.

In her book, *Waiting for a Miracle*, Jan Markell writes, "There are days when laughter can only spring up within us as a gift from God."[5] The key is to focus on the Lord and be attentive to the gifts of laughter he brings into our lives.

Serious by nature, I must work to incorporate God's gift of laughter into my life. I value the perspective of friends who laugh easily, who enable me to glean humor even when I'm exhausted. Humorous books are within easy reach on my bookshelf. When in pain, I often borrow comedies from our library's video collection. And of course, if all else fails, there's always my laugh box.

Lord, thank you for the gift of laughter that brings healing to my body and spirit.

"I believe that laughter is a sacred sound to our God. I also believe that it has an incredible capacity to heal our bodies, our minds, and our spirits."[6]

—TIM HANSEL

Rest for the Weary

For he grants sleep to those he loves.

—PSALM 127:2

Rest Stops

"Come with me by yourselves to a quiet place and get some rest." (Mark 6:31)

My eyes retraced the pattern on the ceiling. I stretched my aching legs and adjusted my position in bed for the umpteenth time. Extreme weakness and the side effects of a new seizure medication sentenced me to a time of prolonged bed rest. My world shrank smaller and smaller until I wondered—*Is there life beyond these bedroom walls?*

Like the child who outwardly obeys but inwardly rebels, my body screamed, *Stop!*, but my mind ran on overload. Feeling lazy and useless, I refused to give myself permission to relax.

Our society thrives on productivity. We tend to view rest—the cessation of activity—as laziness. Regardless of how vital and legitimate the need for rest, guilt seeps into our minds. We plead, *Lord, just let me finish one more task. Then, if I have time, I'll rest.*

Yet even Jesus, engaged in vibrant ministry, understood the necessity of drawing aside for rest. In Mark 6, the disciples ministered nonstop as they preached, drove out demons, and healed the sick. Recognizing their need for a break, Jesus urged the disciples to come with him to a "quiet place and get some rest" (Mark 6:31).

Rest stops provide times of physical and spiritual refreshment. Away from the clatter and demands of life, we can recharge our bodies. Our ability to focus on our relationship with the Lord sharpens when distractions and activities are set aside. We aren't Energizer bunnies. Nor are rest stops simply blank spaces in the patterns of our lives. God created the need for rest into the rhythm of our bodies. He also places rest stops at just the right locations in our spiritual journey. For when we are resting, God is allowed to be active in our lives.

As I lay in bed staring at the ceiling, I reminded myself that God rested after he created the world. If God, my Creator, recognized the value of rest, shouldn't I acknowledge my need for rest as well? It was a good thought as I lay there. And as I pondered this thought, tension oozed out of my body. With a sigh, I finally accepted God's permission to relax.

Lord, help me to recognize rest stops as gifts from you. Thank you for times of rest and refreshment.

"My body also will rest secure." (Ps. 16:9)

Prescription for Weariness

*"Come to me, all you who are weary and burdened, and
I will give you rest. Take my yoke upon you and learn
from me, for I am gentle and humble in heart, and you
will find rest for your souls. For my yoke is easy
and my burden is light."* (Matt. 11:28–30)

I gulped ragged breaths as I stood before the audience of
parents. Lugging tubs of books and setting up for the presentation had exhausted my small reserve of energy. Tears
of pain and frustration filled my eyes. I struggled to regain my
composure.

*Lord, it's too much! I'm sick and tired of being sick and tired
all the time.*

I stumble under the load of frightening symptoms, medical
tests, and painful treatments. My life is controlled by weariness
so severe that it hurts. I drag myself through work responsibilities and feel guilty because I do an inadequate job. How I long
to take a vacation from my sick and weary body!

Good news! You and I don't have to carry this burden of illness alone. The Lord invites us to "come" to him. We draw near to the Lord by spending time with him. We *come* to him through prayer and through reading and meditating on his Word.

As we come to him in the quietness of our souls, the Lord replaces exhaustion with sweet rest. His yoke is custom-made to fit our particular situations. When we share this load with him, he carries the heaviest weight of the yoke for us. We find refreshment for our souls as the Lord walks along beside us.

No, we can't desert our bodies and run off to a mountain cabin for rest and relaxation. We can't take a pill for weariness. There isn't an earthly antidote for relieving the heavy weight of illness. But as we *come* to the Lord, he shares our burden and refreshes our souls. In him, we have the perfect prescription for weariness. And what an easy pill to swallow!

Lord, sometimes I ache with weariness. The burden of my illness is more than my weak shoulders can bear. Thank you for carrying the heaviest part of my load. Thank you that your "yoke is easy" and "your burden is light."

Praise be to the Lord, to God our Savior, who daily bears our burdens. (Ps. 68:19)

Life in the Slow Lane

The Lord is my shepherd, I shall not be in want.
He makes me lie down in green pastures,
he leads me beside quiet waters. (Ps. 23:1, 2)

Cathy zoomed down life's highway toward the title of Super Mom. She chauffeured her children to volleyball games, choir practice, and a myriad of other activities. Earning her associate degree demanded hours of class time and study. Since her husband worked nights, Cathy's lifestyle mirrored that of a single mom.

A slave to her frantic pace, Cathy relegated God to the back recesses of her mind—worthy of a passing thought now and then. She only attended church for Easter and Christmas services. There wasn't time to squeeze anything else into her busy schedule.

Cathy's whirlwind of activity came to a sudden halt when she began to experience severe, unpredictable migraine headaches accompanied by nausea. With each migraine, she was certain someone was hammering on both sides of her head with a mallet. Bright light would sting her eyes and amplify the pounding in her head. Soon Cathy would retreat to a darkened room. She would put an ice pack on her forehead and another behind her neck to relieve some of the pressure and pain.

Cathy's migraines thrust her into the slow lane of life. The joy of accompanying her daughter on choir tours ended. She cheered her daughter's volleyball victories from home. Although she eventually graduated with her associate degree, her illness destroyed her dreams of a promotion and a high-paying job.

Yet, not all was lost. As time has passed and she has adjusted to a slower pace, Cathy finds that the slow lane offers benefits of its own. The greatest benefit comes in her relationship with the Lord. She enjoys God's grace—and has time for it.

Cathy also recognizes the value of savoring each moment—to capture the joy in the little things: a short walk in the sunshine, time to reach out to others, and the pleasure of waking up on a pain-free morning. Preferring the richness of her life in the slow lane, she never plans to return to the Super Mom track.

Although sometimes we prefer to ride the rapids, God often has other plans. We are refreshed as we slow down and rest near his restorative streams. In the calm, he ministers to our deepest needs.

Our culture tempts us with its hurried pace. But the true joy of living is found in the slow lane.

Father, quiet my heart and mind. Help me to slow down and savor each moment you have given me.

"Slow me down, Lord! Ease the pounding of my heart by the quieting of my mind. Steady my hurried pace with a vision of the eternal reach of time."[1]

—WILFERD A. PETERSON

A Time to Be Still

"Be still, and know that I am God." (Ps. 46:10)

Nanette stood at the kitchen sink washing the evening dishes for her family of six. Relentless pain enveloped her body—the result of yet another flare-up of rheumatoid arthritis. A moan escaped her lips as she placed a dish in the rack.

The moaning drew her husband, Jim, back into the kitchen. He insisted Nanette sit and do nothing while he finished the dishes. She shuffled into the living room.

The splashing of water and clinking of dishes tore at Nanette's heart. *Do nothing? How many times must Jim come home from a long day at work and complete my household responsibilities?*

Be still. The very words project a negative image. We thrive on action and busyness. Perceiving stillness as a vacuum, we hurry to fill it. As Christians, most of us possess an innate desire to serve the Lord and others. We feel worthless and passive when we are forced to sit and watch others accomplish *our* tasks.

Yet sometimes, God calls us to stillness. Refusing to shout, he strips away the noise of busyness and distractions so we can better hear his voice. Then, like a camera lens zoomed in on a single object, we can focus on God with amazing clarity.

In Psalm 46:10, we are directed to "be still" in order to "know" God. How do we become better acquainted with someone? We get to know a person by spending time with him. In the same way, our relationship with God deepens and grows during quiet times alone with him. We move from knowing *about* God in our minds to *knowing* him in our hearts.

Stillness is an often-overlooked gift of illness. From the quiet of our beds and couches, we can affect eternity for God through our prayers. The depth of our knowledge of and relationship with God is all the sweeter for having been forged through times of forced respite.

Be still—a very unnatural state. However, for our physical, emotional, and spiritual health, times of stillness can be an unexpected blessing.

Father, thank you for the gift of stillness. Rather than rushing to fill the quiet with noise, may I fill it with you.

I do not concern myself with great matters
or things too wonderful for me.
But I have stilled and quieted my soul;
like a weaned child with its mother,
like a weaned child is my soul within me. (Ps. 131:1, 2)

A Thief Named Worry

*"Who of you by worrying can add a single hour to his life?
Since you cannot do this very little thing, why do
you worry about the rest?"* (Luke 12:25, 26)

*Cast all your anxiety on him because
he cares for you.* (1 Pet. 5:7)

I watched in horror as the mercury soared up the blood-pressure monitor. My blood pressure registered an all-time high. "Are you experiencing any unusual anxiety or stress?" inquired my doctor.

Guilty. Worry, a favorite persistent habit, exposed itself in my rising blood pressure and rapid heart rate. *Will I feel well enough to continue working? What happens if the insurance company won't authorize my expensive medication? Will I finish writing this book by the deadline?* If no glaring worries loom on the horizon, my vivid imagination concocts a few.

Worry is not a benign habit. Anxiety sucks our limited health and strength, erodes our faith in the Lord, and robs us of the gift of today. Health studies indicate that worry possibly steals hours from our lives—just as Jesus implied in Luke 12:25. How do we capture and restrain this elusive thief?

Prayer is our best security system against the thievery of worry. In Philippians 4:6, Paul tells us, "Do not be anxious about anything, but in everything, by prayer and petition, with thanksgiving, present your requests to God." We have a loving Father who waits for us to "cast" our worries on him in prayer (1 Pet. 5:7).

The sources of most of our worries are beyond our control. But by clutching concerns and repeatedly chewing them over in our minds, we waste precious energy. We demonstrate a lack of trust in the Lord. Yet when we transform our worries into prayers, we place control back in God's hands—where it belongs.

One Christmas, a friend who knows me well gave me a small plaque. This plaque sits on my nightstand—a daily reminder to give my concerns to the Lord. The words on this plaque shoot arrows at my worry habit and remind me who's really in control of my life:

> "Good morning, this is God! I will be handling all your problems today and will not need your help. So have a great day!"
>
> —AUTHOR UNKNOWN

Father, forgive me for allowing worry to erode my relationship with you. Thank you for caring about every detail of my life.

"Worry does not empty tomorrow of its sorrow; it empties today of its strength."[2]

—CORRIE TEN BOOM

Songs in the Night

On my bed I remember you;
I think of you through the watches of the night.
Because you are my help,
I sing in the shadow of your wings.
My soul clings to you;
your right hand upholds me. (Ps. 63:6–8)

And His song will be with me in the night,
A prayer to the God of my life. (Ps. 42:8 NASB)

Karen rolled over in yet another futile attempt to find a comfortable position in bed. For over two hours, sleep had eluded her. As she tossed and turned, Karen's ears were tuned to familiar night sounds: her husband brushing his teeth, her teenage sons returning home, and their habitual late-night trips to the refrigerator. Soon, her husband climbed into bed. Within minutes, his rhythmic breathing told an envious Karen he'd fallen asleep. Karen huddled under the covers with her anxious thoughts and ruthless companion—pain.

In the dark watches of the night, the reality of illness balloons, and we wrestle with thoughts and fears that lie dormant in the light of day. *How will I feel tomorrow? What will my latest x-ray show? Will I have an adverse reaction to the new medication?*

Hope dims. The harder we try to fall asleep, the more we toss and turn. If we do slip into sleep, pain jerks us awake.

Pain is not our only companion on sleepless nights. The Lord is with us in each toss and turn, ministering to us with his unique songs in the night. Sometimes we recall verses of Scripture that comfort and encourage us. Other times, we may turn on the light and find rest and peace by reading from his Word. In the lonely stillness of the night, our conversations with the Lord often grow into precious times of intimacy with him. It's as though God eases a cozy blanket over our concerns as we lift our prayers in soft whispers.

As the night wore on, Karen reflected on her many late-night conversations with the Lord. Tears of joy escaped the corners of her eyes as she recalled God's answers to her midnight prayers. Karen's troubled fifteen-year-old son was happier now, her family miraculously restored. She saw God working in the lives of friends for whom she'd prayed during the darkest hours of the night.

The melody, "*Abba, I love you*," resonated in Karen's heart as, at last, she drifted off to sleep.

Lord, thank you for the gift of songs in the darkest night. May the melody of my heart ring with love and gratitude as I rest in you.

"It is easy to sing when we can read the notes by daylight; but it takes a skillful singer whose song springs forth when there is not a ray of light to read by. No man can make a song in the night by himself; he may attempt it, but he will find that a song in the night must be divinely inspired. . . . Since our Maker gives *songs in the night*, let us wait upon Him for the music."[3]

—CHARLES H. SPURGEON

Eyes toward Heaven

"He will wipe every tear from their eyes. There will be no more death or mourning or crying or pain, for the old order of things has passed away."

—REVELATION 21:4

Running the Race

*Therefore, since we are surrounded by such a great cloud
of witnesses, let us throw off everything that hinders and the
sin that so easily entangles, and let us run with perseverance
the race marked out for us. Let us fix our eyes on Jesus,
the author and perfecter of our faith.* (Heb. 12:1, 2)

*I have fought the good fight, I have finished
the race, I have kept the faith.* (2 Tim. 4:7)

The cheers of the crowd roared in Sue's ears. Adrenaline
shot through her body. Her heart pounded in anticipation as she stood in position at the starting line. Months
of discipline, determination, and training had brought her to
this moment.

Bang! Sue pressed forward—lost in the sea of runners. She
concentrated on establishing steady rhythmic breathing while at
the same time resisting the urge to set too fast a pace. Soon she
fell in sync with another runner, allowing her partner to set the
pace for both of them.

Sue's eyes searched hungrily for the signpost markers along
the course. The distance to the finish line was daunting. Each
marker she passed signified another milestone toward the end

of the race. Twenty-six miles later, exhausted but victorious, Sue crossed the finish line.

Now, one year later, Sue is competing in the most grueling race of her life. After months of an array of troubling symptoms, debilitating fatigue, and a marathon of tests, she was diagnosed with mixed connective tissue disease—an autoimmune system disorder. On bad days, a shuffle replaces her sprint. Her endurance plummets.

In his book *Struck Down But Not Destroyed!*, Douglas Wiegand states, "The coping skills required in order to endure chronic illnesses are the same as those needed by a marathon runner."[1] We need fortitude, endurance, and discipline—all qualities of a distance runner—to cope with the demands of illness.

Sue once concentrated on signposts and finish lines. Now her eyes are fixed on the Lord. He entered her in this chronic-illness marathon—marking out the race before her. As she focuses on him, one day the Lord's grace and love will thrust her over the finish line.

Many times illnesses resemble relentless marathons. Hurting bodies beg us to quit the race long before the finish line. We stumble, barely putting one tired foot in front of the other. We fall. It seems as though someone keeps moving the finish line far beyond our reach. This race of our lives requires every ounce of our grit and determination. But as we press on, "fixing our eyes on Jesus," one day we will triumphantly cross the finish line into the welcoming arms of our Lord.

Lord, forgive me for the times I want to quit this chronic-illness marathon. Help me to keep my eyes focused on you as I run with perseverance the race marked out for me.

"The Christian life isn't a hundred-yard dash. It's a marathon."[2]

—STEVE FARRAR, *FINISHING STRONG*

Tents Are Temporary

Now we know that if the earthly tent we live in is destroyed,
we have a building from God, an eternal house in heaven,
not built by human hands. Meanwhile we groan, longing
to be clothed with our heavenly dwelling. (2 Cor. 5:1, 2)

Dark, angry clouds churned beyond the reach of the towering redwood trees. As we drew close to the lake, raindrops splashed on the windshield of the car. Flashes of lightning lit up the sky. The first clap of thunder exploded in our ears, forcing us to return to our campsite along the river. Our swim would have to wait for another day.

Back at camp, we sought refuge inside our tent. The howling wind shook the tent as rain beat a brisk staccato against the canvas. Hailstones hammered on the tent, overpowering the noise of the wind and rain. Something wet struck my back. I glanced behind me just in time to see another golf ball-sized hailstone puncture the side of our tent. Soon the tent was peppered with holes. Water flooded the floor.

Still dressed in our bathing suits, we used bowls, pans, and a bucket in a futile attempt to bail water out of the tent. It was no use. Our tent was ruined.

113

Many times my body reminds me of that flimsy tent. Just when one symptom abates, another pelts my body. Weakness and pain tear the canvas of my feeble frame. This body was *not* made to last.

How I rejoice in God's promise that my physical body is temporary! One day I'll exchange this "perishable" earthly body for a heavenly "imperishable" one (1 Cor. 15:42–44)—a body designed for heaven and made to last forever.

The true nature of our heavenly bodies is one of God's special mysteries—a surprise awaiting us in heaven. But even in my finite mind, I picture strong, healthy bodies. No aching joints. No need for endless hours of rest. We'll walk and run—free from the hindrances of disease.

Best of all, Christ will "transform our lowly bodies so that they will be like his glorious body" (Phil. 3:21). Just imagine, we will bear the likeness of Christ. Our new forms will be perfectly fit for heaven.

Here on earth, we groan as illness assaults our flawed tents. But one day, our pain will end. We will shed these frail bodies. Until then, remember—tents are only temporary.

> *Lord, thank you for the promise that one day I will trade my imperfect body for a glorious heavenly one. Help me to be patient as I eagerly await my new home.*

"He [Paul] knew that death was simply taking down the tent and moving into glorious new quarters."[3]

—WARREN W. WIERSBE

The Shadow of Death

When the perishable has been clothed with the imperishable, and the mortal with immortality, then the saying that is written will come true: "Death has been swallowed up in victory."

"Where, O death, is your victory?
Where, O death, is your sting?"

But thanks be to God! He gives us the victory through our Lord Jesus Christ. (1 Cor. 15:54, 55, 57)

Harry, you have run out of time."

Although these weren't the doctor's exact words, Harry knew he'd just been handed a death sentence. Lou Gehrig's Disease (ALS) is a fatal illness. In a solemn voice, his doctor painted a devastating picture of the disease's expected progression. First, Harry would lose his voice. Then the disease would project its tentacles throughout his body until he would be able to do nothing but breathe. Finally, his diaphragm would fail, leading to death. Harry cried for days.

All of us live under the shadow of death—even though the shadow may not hover as closely over us as over Harry. Death is the one appointment we all must keep. We are powerless to overcome it. As humans, our greatest fear is the fear of our own mortality. Our anguish is rooted in the fear of stepping into the unknown. What does dying feel like? What happens the moment we die? We dread the possibility of enduring pain and suffering at the end of our lives.

But as Christians journeying through the valley of the shadow of death, we can rejoice for Christ has vanquished its sting. Satan and death have been defeated. Because Christ has won the ultimate victory, we have hope beyond the grave.

Yes, death casts a long, frightening shadow over our lives. It is the most terrifying valley through which we will ever travel. But death is not the end. It is our path to Eternity. We have the promise of the Lord's guiding presence as we walk along this path. And best of all, God is waiting for us on the other side of death's shadowy valley—ready to welcome us home.

Heavenly Father, replace my fear of death with the anticipation of eternity with you. Thank you that death isn't the end, but rather it is the pathway to a new beginning.

Even though I walk through the valley of the shadow of death, I will fear no evil, for you are with me; your rod and your staff, they comfort me. (Ps. 23:4)

Hanging on to Hope

We who have fled to take hold of the hope offered to us
may be greatly encouraged. We have this hope as an
anchor for the soul, firm and secure. (Heb. 6:18, 19)

The door closed behind me with a resounding thud. I shuddered as, with the turning of a key, I was locked in the mental health unit of a local hospital.

The nurse searched my belongings and left me alone in the cold, sterile room. Waves of terror and despair swept over me. *How could this happen to me? I'm a Christian! Christians don't get depressed.*

My well-ordered world crumbled. The security of friends and my ability to perform my job were gone. Most dangerous of all, hope slipped from my heart like grains of sand through my fingers. Believing I had nothing left to live for or look forward to, I dwelled in the deepest, blackest pit of my life.

Loss of hope is a hallmark of depression. We survive on hope. Without hope, over time we perish—spiritually, emotionally, and sometimes even physically. Hope and faith are intertwined. When we lose hope, our faith wavers, and we slide down a devastating hill toward unbelief.

We can't manufacture hope. Hope is a gift from God—rooted in his character and based on his promises. Since God is truth, we are assured that all of his promises are true. The hope we place in earthly things and people falters. The hope we place in God is firm and secure—as solid as an anchor (Heb. 6:19).

In time, prayer, a deepening trust in the Lord, and Christian counseling fanned into flame the embers of hope in my heart. Through this experience, I also learned to recognize the danger signs of depression. I learned to cling to my hope in the Lord with everything I had. Reading God's precious promises in the Bible helps me to continue to hang on to my hope.

Depression often accompanies chronic illness. It may be a symptom of a chronic disease or a response to the realities of living with an ongoing illness. Lack of a clear diagnosis, continual pain, and the side effects of medication threaten to devour the hope of even the strongest of us. Contrary to popular belief, Christians are not immune to depression.

But our hope isn't in our fluctuating circumstances and emotions. It is a rock-solid hope in the living Lord. So, hang on, and don't let go!

Father, thank you for the solid, unwavering hope I have in Christ. In the most hopeless of circumstances, may I cling to my eternal hope in you.

May the God of hope fill you with all joy and peace as you trust in him, so that you may overflow with hope by the power of the Holy Spirit. (Rom. 15:13)

The Big Picture

Therefore we do not lose heart. Though outwardly we are
wasting away, yet inwardly we are being renewed day by day.
For our light and momentary troubles are achieving for us an
eternal glory that far outweighs them all. So we fix our eyes
not on what is seen, but on what is unseen. For what is seen
is temporary, but what is unseen is eternal. (2 Cor. 4:16–18)

I focused the lens of my small camera on the San Juan Islands
that pockmark the waters of Puget Sound. There was no
way my camera could ever capture the beautiful expanse of
water and islands—even from this outlook high above Orcas
Island. I settled for a snapshot of just a portion of the beautiful
surroundings. But when I set my camera down and stepped
back, my eyes feasted on the complete picture of water, islands,
and mountain peaks.

When pain and fatigue strike, the camera lens of my thoughts
and emotions zooms in on my illness. Nothing else reaches my
field of vision. The snapshot of my life consists of intense suffering and despair. I lose heart.

In 2 Corinthians 4:16–18, Paul encourages us to view our suffering through the wide lens of eternity. He isn't belittling our hurt. Paul is exhorting us to step back and look at our illnesses in light of the big picture—to see our illnesses from God's perspective.

Looking through God's lens, we realize our suffering is temporary. Meanwhile, the suffering we endure is "achieving for us an eternal glory . . ." (2 Cor. 4:17). Our pain is minuscule compared to the magnificence of the glory awaiting us. This eternal perspective gives us strength.

I gain God's perspective by reading and meditating on his Word. Verses such as 2 Corinthians 4:16–18 are plastered in my mind as well as on my bedroom wall. When pain and fatigue overwhelm me, I focus my mind and heart on the big picture conveyed in these verses.

Yes, my body is wasting away. My illness feels anything but "light" or "momentary." It's easy to zoom in on my suffering. Healing and relief may not happen during my earthly life. But I know not to lose heart. On a daily basis, God is renewing me on the inside. He can do the same for you. Our deepest pain is gaining great glory in the light of eternity.

This is the big picture—through God's lens.

Lord, so often I can't see past my pain. Help me to step back and view my frail body in light of eternity.

"Eternity is the frame around the picture of a life that simply will not make sense without it."[4]

—PAULA RINEHART

Welcome Home!

"Do not let your hearts be troubled. Trust in God;
trust also in me. In my Father's house are many rooms;
if it were not so, I would have told you. I am going there to
prepare a place for you. And if I go and prepare a place
for you, I will come back and take you to be with me
that you also may be where I am." (John 14:1–3)

Yes! Lisa ripped open the envelope. Excitement stirred as she read the invitation.

This party had been on her calendar for months. Arthritis dictated the necessity of flat, sensible shoes. However, she'd purchased a lovely new outfit for the occasion.

On the day of the party, Lisa awoke with a severe flare-up of rheumatoid arthritis. As much as she longed to push herself and attend the party, her stubborn, aching body refused to obey. Once again, the disappointment of canceling long-anticipated plans stung Lisa.[5]

There is one party Lisa and the rest of us won't miss— our homecoming party in heaven. Even now, Jesus is preparing our home for us. Our finite, mortal minds can't begin to comprehend the wonder and beauty of heaven. Yet as magnificent as heaven will be, the glory of worshiping in the actual presence of our Lord will outshine it all.

Are you homesick for heaven? God has placed eternity in our hearts (Eccles. 3:11)—a hunger unsatisfied by anything here on earth. These are good hunger pains. They remind us that this earth is not our home and that our suffering is temporary. On pain-filled days, we can cling to this restless yearning for heaven.

The day of our homecoming party draws nearer with each passing breath. Soon we will dwell with our King forever. Until that day, we can live our earthly lives in anticipation of all that awaits us in our true, heavenly home. What a celebration that will be!

And Lisa? Look for the woman dressed in the new outfit *and* wearing high-heeled shoes!

Lord, when the pain and discouragement of life on earth threaten to overwhelm me, remind me that I'm just a sojourner here. May I live in anticipation of my homecoming party in heaven.

"Home tugs on the heart. . . . I believe that God put the desire for home into our hearts to point us toward something larger and greater—that we belong in the Father's house."[6]

—HARRY ADAMS

Notes

Section 1: By God's Design

1. Ruth Myers, quoted in Carole Mayhall, *When God Whispers: Glimpses of an Extraordinary God by an Ordinary Woman* (Colorado Springs: NavPress, 1994), 20.

2. Cynthia Heald, *Abiding in Christ* (Colorado Springs: NavPress, 1995), 70.

3. Excerpted from *31 Days of Praise,* p. 51. © 1994 by Warren and Ruth Myers. Used by permission of Multnomah Publishers, Inc.

4. John Wesley, quoted in Charles R. Swindoll, *The Tale of the Tardy Oxcart and 1,501 Other Stories* (Nashville: W Publishing Group, 1998), 534.

Section 2: Strength for the Journey

1. Taken from: *Minute Meditations for Healing and Hope,* p. 165. Copyright © 2003 by Emilie Barnes. Published by Harvest House Publishers, Eugene, OR. Used by permission.

2. Dwight L. Moody, quoted in Tony Castle, comp., *The New Book of Christian Quotations* (New York: Crossroad, 1982), 232.

3. Warren W. Wiersbe, *The Bumps Are What You Climb On* (Grand Rapids, MI: Baker Books, Baker Book House Company, 2002), 12. Used by permission of Baker Book House Company.

Section 3: The Furnace of Affliction

1. Lynn Eib is the author of *When God and Cancer Meet,* Wheaton, IL: Tyndale House, 2002. Her Web site for cancer patients and caregivers is www.CancerPatientAdvocate.com.

2. Jan Markell, *Waiting for a Miracle* (Grand Rapids, MI: Baker Books, Baker Book House Company, 1993), 67. Used by permission of author.

3. C.S. Lewis, *The Problem of Pain* (New York: HarperSanFrancisco, 2001), 91. Extract reprinted by permission of C. S. Lewis Pte. Ltd. © 1940, 1960.

4. Dr. and Mrs. Howard Taylor, *Hudson Taylor's Spiritual Secret* (Chicago: Moody, 1989), 152. Used by permission of Moody Publishers.

5. Selwyn Hughes, *The Divine Gardener* (Surrey, England: Crusade for World Revival, 2001), 2. Used by permission of Crusade for World Revival.

6. John Henry Jowett, quoted in Mark Water, comp., *The New Encyclopedia of Christian Quotations* (Grand Rapids, MI: Baker Books, Baker Book House Company, 2000), 211.

7. Charles R. Swindoll, *For Those Who Hurt* (1977; repr., Grand Rapids, MI: Zondervan, 1977), 17. Used by permission of author.

Section 4: Through Deep Waters

1. Carole Mayhall, *Help Lord, I'm Sinking: Lessons from My Rocking Boat* (Colorado Springs: NavPress, 1997), 69.

2. Ibid.

3. George Sweeting, *Who Said That?* (Chicago: Moody, 1995), 161. Used by permission of Moody Publishers.

Section 5: Courage in the Darkness

1. Jan Coleman, *After the Locusts* (Nashville: Broadman & Holman, 2002), 65. Used by permission of Broadman & Holman Publishers.

2. Tim Hansel, *You Gotta Keep Dancin'* (Colorado Springs: Life Journey, 2004), 106. Used by permission of Cook Communications Ministries.

3. Charles H. Spurgeon, *Morning and Evening,* rev. by Alistair Begg (Wheaton, IL: Crossway, 2003), October 17, Morning. Used by permission of Crossway Books.

4. Ibid., July 8, Evening.

5. Corrie ten Boom, *A Prisoner and Yet . . .* 2nd American ed. (Fort Washington, PA: Christian Literature Crusade, 1996), 44. Used by permission of Fleming H. Revell, Baker Book House Company.

Section 6: Springs in the Desert

1. John Wimber, "Signs, Wonders, and Cancer," *Christianity Today,* 40, no. 11 (October 7, 1966): 50. Used by permission of Sean and Christy Wimber.

2. Henri J. M. Nouwen, *Reaching Out: The Three Movements of the Spiritual Life* (New York: Image, 1986), 34.

3. Christina Smith, quoted in Lynn Vanderzalm, *Spiritual Sunlight for the Weary* (Colorado Springs: WaterBrook Press, 1998), 19. All rights reserved. Used by permission of WaterBrook Press.

4. Excerpted from *The Glorious Intruder,* p. 48. © 1989 by Joni Eareckson Tada. Used by permission of Multnomah Publishers Inc.

5. Markell, 53.

6. Hansel, 81.

Section 7: Rest for the Weary

1. Wilferd A. Peterson, *Adventures in the Art of Living* (New York: Simon & Schuster, 1968), 58, 59. Used by permission of Heacock Literary Agency, Inc.

2. Corrie ten Boom, *Clippings from My Notebook* (Minneapolis: World Wide Publications, 1982), 33. Used by permission of Fleming H. Revell, Baker Book House Company.

3. Spurgeon, *Morning and Evening,* October 19, Evening.

Section 8: Eyes toward Heaven

1. Douglas Wiegand, *Struck Down But Not Destroyed! A Christian's Response to Chronic Illness and Pain* (Baden, PA: Rainbow's End, 1996), 21. Used by permission of author.

2. Excerpted from *Finishing Strong*, p. 21. © 1995 by Steve Farrar. Used by permission of Multnomah Publishers Inc.

3. Wiersbe, 21. Used by permission of Baker Book House Company.

4. Paula Rinehart, "Living in Light of Eternity," *Discipleship Journal*, no. 136 (July/August, 2003): 52. Used by permission of author.

5. Lisa Copen is the director of Rest Ministries, an international Christian support ministry for those with chronic illness. Their Web site may be found at www.restministries.org.

6. Harry A. Adams, *God, I Want to Ask You: Seven Questions When Facing Death* (Kearney, NE: Morris, 2000), 42.

Resources of Comfort and Encouragement

Copen, Lisa. *Mosaic Moments: Devotionals for the Chronically Ill.*
San Diego: Rest Ministries Publishers, 2002.
 A collection of devotionals written by people who suffer
from chronic illnesses.

Eib, Lynn. *When God and Cancer Meet.* Wheaton, IL: Tyndale
House Publishers, 2002.
 The author, a cancer patient advocate, tells her story and that
of other cancer patients in a powerful book of hope and trust in
God through all phases of cancer.

Givler, Amy. *Hope in the Face of Cancer: A Survival Guide for the
Journey You Did Not Choose.* Eugene, OR: Harvest House
Publishers, 2003.
 The author, a physician and cancer survivor, has written the
book she wanted to read when she was first diagnosed with cancer. Along with her professional expertise, she shares how to find
hope in the midst of a devastating disease.

Hansel, Tim. *You Gotta Keep Dancin': In the Midst of Life's Hurts You Can Choose Joy!* Second printing. Colorado Springs: Life Journey, Cook Communications Ministries, 2004.

Pain is unavoidable in this life. But misery is optional! Tim Hansel, who's lived with continual pain for over twenty years, explains how to choose joy in the midst of the most painful life circumstances.

Padrick, Stacey. *Living with Mystery: Finding God in the Midst of Unanswered Questions.* Minneapolis: Bethany House Publishers, 2001.

Stacey Padrick shows us how to trust God and grow spiritually in the face of unanswered questions. Stacey, who suffers from lupus, shares from her experience in *God of All Comfort.* You can order Stacey's book by contacting her at Livingwmystery@aol.com.

Tada, Joni Eareckson, and Steven Estes. *When God Weeps.* Grand Rapids, MI: Zondervan, 2000.

Joni Eareckson Tada is a quadriplegic who has been in a wheelchair for over thirty years. This book tackles hard questions about suffering and why God allows it in our lives.

Wiersbe, Warren. *The Bumps Are What You Climb On.* Grand Rapids: Baker Books, Baker Book House Company, 2002.

Meditations to encourage us to view the difficult situations in life as "bumps" to climb—on the road to spiritual growth.

Yancey, Philip. *Where Is God When It Hurts?* rev. ed. Grand Rapids, MI: Zondervan, 1990.

In this classic on the topic of suffering, Philip Yancey discusses the age-old question: Why does God allow suffering? Using examples from the Bible and his own experiences, the author looks at pain from God's perspective and helps us understand why we suffer.